Study Guide for the Spanish Tests

▶ ▶ ▶ ▶ ▶ ▶ ▶ ▶ ▶ ▶ ▶ ▶ ▶

A PUBLICATION OF ETS

Copyright © 2005 by Educational Testing Service. All rights reserved.
EDUCATIONAL TESTING SERVICE, ETS, the ETS logo, GRE, and THE PRAXIS SERIES: PROFESSIONAL ASSESSMENTS FOR
BEGINNING TEACHERS are registered trademarks of Educational Testing Service. SAT is a registered trademark of the College Entrance
Examination Board. THE PRAXIS SERIES is a trademark of Educational Testing Service.

Table of Contents
Study Guide for the Spanish Tests

▶ ▶ ▶ ▶ ▶ ▶ ▶ ▶ ▶ ▶ ▶ ▶

TABLE OF CONTENTS

Chapter 1
Introduction to the Spanish Tests and Suggestions for Using This Study Guide 1

Chapter 2
Background Information on The Praxis Series™ Subject Assessments 5

Chapter 3
Study Topics—*Spanish: Content Knowledge* 9

Chapter 4
Succeeding on Multiple-Choice Questions 27

Chapter 5
Practice Questions—*Spanish: Content Knowledge* 37

Chapter 6
Right Answers and Explanations for the Practice
Questions—*Spanish: Content Knowledge* 71

Chapter 7
Preparing for *Spanish: Productive Language Skills* 83

Chapter 8
Succeeding on Constructed-Response Questions 97

Chapter 9
Practice Questions—*Spanish: Productive Language Skills* 107

Chapter 10
Sample Responses and How They Were
Scored—*Spanish: Productive Language Skills* 129

Chapter 11
Are You Ready?—Last-Minute Tips 163

Appendix A
Study Plan Sheet 167

Appendix B
For More Information 169

Chapter 1

Introduction to the Spanish Tests and Suggestions for Using This Study Guide

▶   ▶   ▶   ▶   ▶   ▶   ▶   ▶   ▶   ▶   ▶   ▶

Introduction to the Spanish Tests

The Praxis Series™ Spanish tests assess beginning teachers' understanding of the language and the culture of the countries and regions where Spanish is spoken.

The *Spanish: Content Knowledge* test (0191) consists of 120 multiple-choice questions based on recorded and printed materials in Spanish. It covers four major areas, in the following proportions:

Content Category	Approximate Number of Questions	Approximate Percentage of Examination
■ Interpretive Listening (in Spanish)	32	27%
■ Structure of the Language (Grammatical Accuracy, in Spanish and English)	34	28%
■ Interpretive Reading (in Spanish)	31	26%
■ Cultural Perspectives (in Spanish)	23	19%

You have two hours to complete the test.

The test is not intended to assess teaching skills but rather your competence in various language skills and your knowledge of the cultures of Spain and Spanish-speaking countries in Latin America.

The *Spanish: Productive Language Skills* test (0192) consists of nine questions—six questions that you must answer in spoken Spanish (the Presentational Speaking section of the test) and three questions that you must answer in written Spanish (the Presentational Writing section). The test covers these two sections in the following proportions:

Content Category	Number of Questions	Percentage of Total Test Score	Minutes
■ Presentational Speaking	6	60%	25 (approximate)
■ Presentational Writing	3	40%	35

You have one hour to complete the test.

The test is not intended to assess teaching skills but rather your ability to speak and write Spanish.

Suggestions for using this study guide

These language tests are different from final exams or other tests you may have taken for other courses because they are comprehensive—that is, they cover material you may have learned in several courses during your entire undergraduate program. They require you to synthesize information you have learned from many sources and to understand the subject as a whole.

Therefore, you should review and prepare for the test you plan to take, rather than merely becoming familiar with the question formats. A thorough review of the material covered on the test will significantly increase your likelihood of success. Moreover, studying for your licensing exam is a great opportunity to reflect on and develop a deeper understanding of your field before you begin to teach. As you prepare to take the test, it may be particularly helpful for you to think about how you would apply the study topics and sample exercises to the teaching experiences you obtained during your teacher preparation program. Your student teaching experience will be especially relevant to your thinking about the materials in the study guide.

We recommend the following approach for using this study guide to prepare for the test.

Become familiar with the test content. Learn what will be assessed in the test you plan to take, covered in chapter 3 (for the *Spanish: Content Knowledge* test) and chapter 7 (for the *Spanish: Productive Language Skills* test).

Assess how well you know the content in each area. After you learn what topics the test contains, you should assess your knowledge in each area. How well do you know the material? In which areas do you need to learn more before you take the test? It is quite likely that you will need to brush up on most or all of the areas.

Develop a study plan. Assess what you need to study and create a realistic plan for studying. You can develop your study plan in any way that works best for you. A "Study Plan" form is included in appendix A at the end of the book as a possible way to structure your planning. Remember that these are licensure tests that cover a great deal of material. Plan to review carefully. You will need to allow time to find books and other materials, time to read the materials and take notes, and time to go over your notes.

Identify study materials. Most of the materials covered by these tests are contained in standard introductory textbooks. If you do not own introductory texts that cover all the relevant areas, you may want to borrow some from friends or from a library. You may also want to obtain a copy of your state's standards for Spanish. (One way to find these standards quickly is to go to the Web site for your state's Department of Education.) The textbooks used in secondary classrooms may also prove useful to you, since they often present the material you need to know. Use standard school and college introductory textbooks and other reliable, professionally prepared materials. Don't rely heavily on information provided by friends or from searching the World Wide Web. Neither of these sources is as uniformly reliable as textbooks.

Work through your study plan. You may want to work alone, or you may find it more helpful to work with a group or with a mentor. Work through the topics and descriptions of question types outlined in chapters 3 and 7. Rather than memorizing definitions from books, be able to define and discuss the topics and question types in your own words and understand the relationships among diverse topics and concepts. If you are working with a group or mentor, you can also try informal quizzes and questioning techniques.

Learn about the test format in chapters 4 or 8. If you are taking the *Spanish: Content Knowledge* test, read chapter 4 to sharpen your skills in reading and answering multiple-choice questions. To succeed on multiple-choice questions, you must focus carefully on each question, avoid reading things into the question, pay attention to details, and sift patiently through the answer choices. If you are taking the *Spanish: Productive Language Skills* test, read chapter 8 to learn how constructed-response tests are scored. This chapter also contains valuable tips on how to succeed on a test in this format.

Proceed to the practice questions. Once you have completed your review and familiarized yourself with the format for your test, you are ready to benefit from the appropriate "Practice Questions" portions of this guide, chapters 5 and 9.

Suggestions for using the "Practice Questions," "Right Answers," and "Sample Responses" chapters

Answer the practice questions in chapter 5 or 9. Work on the practice questions in a quiet place without distractions. Remember that the practice questions are only examples of the way the topics are covered in the test. The actual test will have different questions.

Score the practice questions. If you have answered the practice questions for the *Spanish*: *Content Knowledge* test, go through the detailed answers in chapter 6, and mark the questions you answered correctly and the ones you missed. Look over the explanations for the correct answers to the questions you missed and see if you understand them. If you have answered the practice questions for the *Spanish*: *Productive Language Skills* test, look in chapter 10 to see sample responses that scored well, scored poorly, or scored in between. By examining these sample responses, you can focus on the aspects of your own practice response that were successful and unsuccessful. This knowledge will help you plan any additional studying you might need.

Decide whether you need more review. After you have looked at your results, decide whether there are areas that you need to brush up on before you take the actual test. Go back to your textbooks and reference materials to see if the topics and skills are covered there. You might also want to go over your questions with a friend or teacher who is familiar with the subjects.

Assess your readiness. Do you feel confident about your level of understanding in each of the areas? If not, where do you need more work? If you feel ready, complete the checklist in chapter 11 ("Are You Ready?—Last-Minute Tips") to double-check that you've thought through the details. If you need more information about registration or the testing situation itself, use the resources in appendix B: "For More Information."

Note: Every effort is made to provide the most recent information in this study guide. However, The Praxis Series tests are continually evaluated and updated. You will always find the most recent information about these tests, including the topics and skills covered, number of questions, time allotted, and scoring criteria, in the *Test at a Glance* booklet available online at http://www.ets.org/praxis/prxtest.html.

Chapter 2
Background Information on The Praxis Series™ Subject Assessments

▶　▶　▶　▶　▶　▶　▶　▶　▶　▶　▶　▶

What Are The Praxis Series Subject Assessments?

The Praxis Series Subject Assessments are designed by ETS to assess your knowledge of specific subject areas. They are a part of the licensing procedure in many states. This study guide covers assessments that test your knowledge of the actual content you will be expected to teach once you are licensed. Your state has adopted The Praxis Series tests because it wants to confirm that you have achieved a specified level of mastery in your subject area before it grants you a license to teach in a classroom.

The Praxis Series tests are part of a national testing program, meaning that the tests covered in this study guide are required in more than one state for licensure. The advantage of a national program is that if you want to move to another state, you can transfer your scores from one state to another. However, each state has specific test requirements and passing scores. If you are applying for a license in another state, you will want to verify the appropriate test and passing score requirements. This information is available online at www.ets.org/praxis/prxstate.html or by calling ETS at 800-772-9476 or 609-771-7395.

What Is Licensure?

Licensure in any area—for example, medicine, law, architecture, accounting, cosmetology—is an assurance to the public that the person holding the license possesses sufficient knowledge and skills to perform important occupational activities safely and effectively. In the case of teacher licensing, a license tells the public that the individual has met predefined competency standards for beginning teaching practice.

Because a license makes such a serious claim about its holder, licensure tests are usually quite demanding. In some fields, licensure tests have more than one part and last for more than one day. Candidates for licensure in all fields plan intensive study as part of their professional preparation: some join study groups, others study alone. But preparing to take a licensure test is, in all cases, a professional activity. Because a licensure exam assesses the entire body of knowledge for the field you are entering, preparing for the test takes planning, discipline, and sustained effort.

Why Does My State Require The Praxis Series Assessments?

Your state chose The Praxis Series assessments because the tests assess the breadth and depth of content—called the "domain"—that your state wants its teachers to possess before they begin to teach. The level of content knowledge, reflected in the passing score, is based on recommendations of panels of teachers and teacher educators in each subject area. The state licensing agency and, in some states, the state legislature ratify the passing scores that have been recommended by panels of teachers.

What Do the Tests Measure?

The Praxis Series Subject Assessments are tests of content knowledge. They measure your understanding and skills in a particular subject area. Multiple-choice tests measure a broad range of knowledge across your content area. Constructed-response tests measure your ability to provide in-depth explanations of a few essential topics in a given subject area. Content-specific pedagogy tests, most of which are constructed response, measure your understanding of how to teach certain fundamental concepts in a subject area. The tests do not measure your actual teaching ability, however. They measure your knowledge of a subject and of how to teach it. The teachers in your field who help us design and write these tests, and the states that require them, do so in the belief that knowledge of your subject area is the first requirement for licensing. Teaching combines many complex skills, only some of which can be measured by a single test. While the tests covered in this study guide measure knowledge of your subject area, your teaching ability is a skill that is typically measured in other ways—for example, through observation, videotaped practice, or portfolios.

How Were These Tests Developed?

ETS began the development of The Praxis Series Subject Assessments with a survey. For each subject, teachers around the country in various teaching situations were asked to judge which knowledge and skills a beginning teacher in that subject needs to possess. Professors in schools of education who prepare teachers were asked the same questions. The responses were ranked in order of importance and sent out to hundreds of teachers for review. All of the responses to these surveys (called "job analysis surveys") were analyzed to summarize the judgments of these professionals. From their consensus, we developed guidelines, or specifications, for the multiple-choice and constructed-response tests. Each subject area had a committee of practicing teachers and teacher educators who wrote the specifications, which were reviewed and eventually approved by teachers. From the test specifications, groups of teachers and professional test developers created test questions that met content requirements and satisfied the *ETS Standards for Quality and Fairness.**

When your state adopted The Praxis Series Subject Assessments, local panels of practicing teachers and teacher educators in each subject area met to examine the tests and to evaluate each question for its relevance to beginning teachers in your state. This is called a "validity study" because local practicing teachers validate that the test content is relevant to the job. For the test to be adopted in your state, teachers in your state must judge that it is valid. During the validity study, the panel also provides a passing-score recommendation. This process includes a rigorous review to determine how many of the test questions a beginning teacher in that state would be able to answer correctly. Your state's licensing agency then reviewed the panel's recommendations and made a final determination of the passing-score requirement.

Throughout the development process, practitioners in the teaching field—teachers and teacher educators— participated in defining what The Praxis Series Subject Assessments would cover, which test would be used for licensure in your subject area, and what score would be needed to achieve licensure. This practice is consistent with how professional licensure works in most fields: those who are already licensed oversee the licensing of new practitioners. When you pass The Praxis Series Subject Assessments, you and the practitioners in your state will have evidence that you have the knowledge and skills required for beginning teaching practice.

---

* *ETS Standards for Quality and Fairness* (2003, Princeton, NJ) are consistent with the "Standards for Educational and Psychological Testing," industry standards issued jointly by the American Educational Research Association, the American Psychological Association, and the National Council on Measurement in Education (1999, Washington, DC).

Chapter 3
Study Topics—*Spanish: Content Knowledge*

▶   ▶   ▶   ▶   ▶   ▶   ▶   ▶   ▶   ▶   ▶   ▶

Introduction to the Test

The Praxis *Spanish: Content Knowledge* test covers understanding of spoken and written Spanish. In some cases, you will be required to answer questions based on recorded conversations and narrations, and in other cases, you will be required to read, interpret, and correct written Spanish. You will also be asked questions about the geography, culture, and history of Spain and Spanish-speaking countries in Latin America.

The purpose of this chapter is to provide guidance on how to prepare for the test. A broad overview of the areas covered in the Praxis *Spanish: Content Knowledge* test is followed by detailed lists of the specific topics that are covered under each broad area.

You are not expected to be an expert on all aspects of the topics that follow. However, you should understand the major characteristics or aspects of each topic and be able to recognize them in various kinds of examples or selections.

Here is an overview of the areas covered on the test, along with their subareas:

Interpretive Listening
27% of the questions

- Short Conversations
- Short Narrations
- Long Conversations and Long Narrations

Structure of the Language
28% of the questions

- Speech Analysis
- Writing Analysis
- Language Analysis
- Grammar Analysis

Interpretive Reading
26% of the questions

- Content and Organization
- Implied Content
- Use of Language

Cultural Perspectives
19% of the questions

- Geography
- Lifestyles and Societies
- Sociolinguistic Elements of Spanish
- History
- Literature and the Arts

Interpretive Listening

This part of the test emphasizes comprehension, interpretation, and analysis of spoken Spanish. The Interpretive Listening section is broken into three subsections: short conversations, short narrations, and long narrations and dialogues. Selections will be read by native speakers of Spanish, followed by questions read orally. Answer choices will appear only in your test book.

Short Conversations

For these questions, you will be asked to listen to a recorded dialogue between two native speakers of Spanish speaking at a normal rate of speech. To complete this task successfully, you must be able to interpret stress and intonation; understand the meanings of key words; understand high-frequency vocabulary, idiomatic expressions, and figures of speech; recognize questions and instructions; understand verb tenses; identify main ideas; and understand conversations about a number of topics.

- Recognize the meaning carried by stress and intonation
  - How does intonation affect meaning?
    - Note that for questions in Spanish, intonation normally rises at the end only with "Yes/No" questions.
  - How do word order and intonation allow you to distinguish questions from statements?

- Understand the meaning of an utterance based on key words
  - How does word order affect meaning?
    - Questions frequently invert order of subject and verb
      — *¿Qué hace Juan? Juan hace su tarea.*
  - What key indicators dictate formal versus informal speech?
    - Use of *tú* versus *usted*

- What verb conjugations indicate different time sequences?
  - Use of imperfect to indicate ongoing or habitual action in the past
    — *De joven, me gustaba ir al cine.*
  - Use of the preterite to indicate a completed, finite occurence in the past
    — *Fui al cine cinco veces en julio.*
- Recognize that associated words can often convey context (e.g., *avión*, *vuelo*, *pasaporte* would indicate a context of international air travel)
- What are common patterns for cognates in English/Spanish?
  - For example, "-ly" endings in English (e.g., "exactly") usually are conveyed by a "*-mente*" ending in Spanish (*exactamente*).

- Understand high-frequency vocabulary, idiomatic expressions, and figures of speech
  - What key idiomatic expressions and figures of speech are essential for learners of Spanish?
  - Understand idiomatic expressions that cannot be translated literally from Spanish to English, such as *¿Qué tal?*, which conveys an informal "How are you?"

- Recognize what question has been asked or what instruction has been given
  - How do you recognize the grammar and intonation associated with commands?

- Understand sentences in the past, present, and future time
  - What key words distinguish the past from the present or the future?
    - Use of the periphrastic future (*ir + a + infinitive*), as in
      — *Voy a decírselo el martes.*
    - Use of certain phrases with past tenses, such as
      — *todos los días* + imperfect
      — *ayer* + preterite

- ▶ What verb conjugations will be important to indicate probability?
  - ◆ Use of the future to express probability in the present or future
    — *Elena estará en su casa.* ("Elena is probably at home.")
- ▶ When is the subjunctive required in Spanish and what does it express?

- ■ Identify the main idea of an informal conversation
  - ▶ Can you determine the main idea through repeated or related words and phrases?
  - ▶ Can you identify a problem, understand a situation, and recognize the resolution of a problem or situation?

- ■ Understand conversations on a variety of everyday topics
  - ▶ Ordering food in a restaurant
  - ▶ Asking for advice
  - ▶ Making a phone call
  - ▶ Talking about entertainment and leisure activities
  - ▶ Discussing health, etc.

Short Narrations

For these questions, you will be asked to listen to one native speaker of Spanish speaking at a normal rate of speech. This person may be telling a brief story, speaking about an event, making an announcement, or providing the type of information you would hear on a radio or television broadcast. To answer these questions successfully, you will use many of the same skills involved in answering questions following short conversations.

- ■ Identify the main idea(s) of nontechnical broadcasts
  - ▶ How can you distinguish a media-type discourse from an informal conversation?

Long Conversations and Long Narrations

For these questions, you will be asked to listen to native speakers of Spanish speaking at a normal rate of speech for an extended period of time, either in extended conversations or longer narrations. To answer these questions successfully, you will use many of the same skills involved in answering questions that follow short conversations or narrations.

Structure of the Language (Grammatical Accuracy)

This section asks you to analyze various aspects of the Spanish language; it encompasses four subcategories. **Speech Analysis** includes identifying and correcting errors in syntax and vocabulary as well as in phonology, such as false cognates. You will hear selections recorded by nonnative Spanish speakers, and you will have to identify their mistakes. **Writing Analysis** asks you to identify, correct, and describe errors in morphology, syntax, and semantics from written selections created by nonnative Spanish speakers. **Language Analysis** tests your knowledge of such aspects of Spanish grammar as verb endings, subject-verb agreement, moods, time, word order, article-noun agreement, noun-adjective agreement, and emphasis. **Grammar Analysis** tests your knowledge of Spanish grammar and your ability to correctly complete sentences within the context of a paragraph or a longer written selection.

Review of the following aspects of the language may be helpful in your preparation for the *Spanish: Content Knowledge* test. Please keep in mind that this is to serve as a guide and is not intended to be an exhaustive description of Spanish grammar and language use.

- Nouns
  - Gender and number agreement
  - Use of lowercase for days of the week and months
  - Use of the personal *a* when direct object pronouns are people or personalized objects
    - *¿Conoces a Marta?*
    - *Quiero mucho a mi perro.*

- Articles
  - Prescribed use of masculine singular article with feminine words that begin with the stressed sound of *a* or *ha* (*el agua, el hacha,* but *las aguas, las hachas*)
  - Use of the definite article before the names of days of the week to indicate "on", e.g., *Luis llega el lunes.* ("Luis arrives on Tuesday.")
  - Contraction of articles: *de + el = del; a + el = al*

- Adjectives (descriptive, possessive, demonstrative)
  - Adjectives expressing beauty, age, goodness, and size usually follow the nouns they modify.
    - *Es un libro largo.* "It is a long book."
  - Certain adjectives change in meaning, depending on whether they precede or follow the nouns they modify (e.g., *Es un viejo amigo* does not convey the same message as *Es un amigo viejo*).
  - When used before nouns, some adjectives are shortened (e.g., *un palacio grande* means "a big palace" whereas *un gran palacio* conveys "a grandiose palace").

- Some adjectives change meaning when used with *ser* or *estar* (e.g., *Es listo* does not convey the same meaning as *Está listo*).

- Comparisons of equality and inequality (of nouns, of adjectives)
  - *más/menos . . . que* but *más/menos . . . de* when followed by a number
    - *Tengo más libros que Ana.*
    - *Tengo más de treinta libros.*

- Pronouns
  - Subject pronouns: *yo, tú, usted (Ud.), él, ella, nosotros, nosotras, vosotros, vosotras, ustedes (Uds.), ellos, ellas*
  - Demonstrative pronouns: *esto, esta, este, ese, esa, aquel, aquella, estos, estas, esos, esas, aquellos, aquellas*

    Note: demonstrative pronouns *este, ese, esta, este, aquel, aquella, estos, estas, esas, esos, aquellos, aquellos* are no longer accented. The meanings of these words, which are spelled the same as demonstrative adjectives, are recognized from context.
  - Possessive pronouns: *el mío, la mía, el tuyo, la tuya, el suyo, la suya, el nuestro, la nuestra, el vuestro, la vuestra, los míos, las mías, los tuyos, las tuyas, los suyos, las suyas, los nuestros, las nuestras, los vuestros, las vuestras*
  - Direct object pronouns: *me, te, lo, la, nos, os, los, las*
  - Indirect object pronouns: *me, te, le, se, nos, os, les*
  - Double object pronouns appear as indirect object pronoun followed by direct object pronoun, whether they precede a conjugated verb or are attached to an infinitive.
    - *Elvira me lo va a dar. / Elvira va a dármelo.*
  - Object pronouns come before a negative command but are attached to an affirmative command.
    - *¡No me hables! / ¡Háblame!*
    - *¡No se lo des! / ¡Dáselo!*

► Reflexive pronouns: *me, te, se, nos, os, se*

► Reflexive pronouns reflect the same person as the subject.

 ◆ *Yo me voy. ¿Ustedes se van?*

► Pronouns used as objects of prepositions: *mí, ti, él, ella, nosotros, nosotras, vosotros, vosotras, ellos, ellas*

 Note: The following pronouns are used as objects of the preposition *con*:

 ◆ *conmigo* ("with me"), *contigo* ("with you"), *consigo* ("with yourself" *[usted/ustedes]*, "with himself," "with herself," "with themselves")

 — *Ven conmigo.*

 — *Lléveselo consigo.*

■ Indefinites and Negatives

► Modifiers: *algún, alguna, algunos, algunas*; *ningún, ninguna, ningunos, ningunas*

 ◆ *Algunos libros están en rebaja.*

 ◆ *Ningún comentario le gustó.*

► Pronouns: *alguno, alguna, algunos, algunas*; *ninguno, ninguna, ningunos, ningunas*; *alguien, nadie*

 ◆ *Aunque oyó muchos comentarios, ninguno le gustó.*

 ◆ *¿Alguien pidió postre? No, nadie pidió postre.*

► Unlike English, Spanish often uses double negatives.

 ◆ *No vino nadie a la fiesta.* ("No one came to the party.")

 ◆ *También, tampoco*

 — *Gabriela vino a la fiesta y su hermana también.* ("Gabriela came to the party and her sister came, too.")

 — *Gabriela no vino a la fiesta; su hermana no vino tampoco.* ("Gabriela didn't come to the party; her sister didn't come, either.")

◆ no . . . ni; ni . . . ni

 — *No vino Gabriela a la fiesta ni su hermana tampoco.* ("Gabriela did not come to the party, and her sister did not either.")

 — *Ni Gabriela ni su hermana vino a la fiesta.* ("Neither Gabriela nor her sister came to the party.")

■ Interrogatives

► Questions in Spanish are opened with an inverted question mark; they end with a regular question mark. (Hint: it is as if the question were surrounded by parentheses; the opening one has a "tail" up and the closing one has a "tail" down.)

 ◆ *María, ¿sabes su dirección?*

► *¿Qué?/¿Cuál?/¿Cuáles?/¿Cómo?/ ¿Dónde?/¿Por qué?/¿Cuándo?/¿Quién?/ ¿Quiénes?*

► Interrogative words take accents in Spanish, even when they are in statements but have interrogative meanings.

 ◆ *Sé quién es el muchacho nuevo pero no sé dónde vive.*

■ Prepositions

► When a verb follows a preposition, the verb appears in the infinitive in Spanish.

 ◆ *Antes de hablar, hay que pensar.* ("Before speaking, one must think.")

► Frequently, verb-preposition combinations do not follow the pattern of English. Verb-preposition combinations in Spanish should be learned as vocabulary for their various meanings.

 ◆ *Pienso en esas vacaciones mucho.* ("I think about that vacation a lot.")

 ◆ *¿Qué piensas de eso?* ("What do you think about that?")

► Use of *por* and *para*

- Adverbs
  - ▶ Adverbs in Spanish are usually formed by adding the ending -*mente* to the feminine singular form of adjectives when the adjectives end in vowels.
    - ◆ *rápido—rápidamente*
    - ◆ *general—generalmente*
  - ▶ Some adverbs are irregular in their formation in Spanish.
    - ◆ *bueno / bien*
      - — *Elena sacó una buena nota en su composición; la redactó bien.* ("Elena got a good grade on her composition; she wrote it well.")

- Verbs
  - ▶ Verbs in Spanish end in -*ar, -er*, and -*ir*. Most verbs follow a regular pattern when conjugated. There are exceptions:
    - ◆ Stem-changing verbs
      - — Some verbs with an *e* or an *o* in their stem will go into an *ie* or *ue* pattern when that vowel is stressed.
        - ▾ *pensar: yo pienso / nosotros pensamos*
        - ▾ *contar: tú cuentas / nosotros contamos*
      - — Some -*ir* verbs with an *e* in their stem will go into an *i* pattern when that vowel is stressed.
        - ▾ *pedir: yo pido / nosotros pedimos*
    - ◆ Spelling-changing verbs
      - — Some verbs change to keep sound patterns.
        - ▾ *seguir: sigo; sigues*
    - ◆ Irregular changes
      - — *ir: voy, vas, va, vamos, vais, van*
      - — *ser: soy, eres, es, somos, sois, son*
    - ◆ Some verbs are irregular in the preterite.
      - — *tener: tuve*
      - — *querer: quise*
  - ◆ Some verbs are irregular in the future and conditional.
    - — *tener: tendré ; tendría*
    - — *salir: saldré; saldría*
    - — *hacer: haré; haría*
  - ◆ Irregular past participles
    - — *abrir / abierto*
    - — *poner / puesto*
  - ▶ Reflexive verbs
    - ◆ Infinitives indicated by attaching *se*
      - — *dormir / dormir(se): Me duermo temprano.*
  - ▶ Use of *ser* versus *estar*
    - ◆ *Soy de Puerto Rico; ¿sabes dónde está?*
  - ▶ Verbs like *gustar*
    - ◆ *Me gusta oír el piano.*
    - ◆ *Le fascina esa orquesta.*
  - ▶ Uses of the simple past tenses (preterite and imperfect) in Spanish
    - ◆ *Estaba comiendo cuando sonó el teléfono.*
    - ◆ *Ayer hubo una tormenta, pero hoy hizo buen tiempo para ir a la playa.*
    - ◆ *Yo siempre fui con ella.* ("I always went with her.")
    - ◆ *Yo siempre iba con ella.* ("I always used to go with her.")
  - ▶ Future and conditional of probability
    - ◆ *¿Dónde está Paco?* ("Where is Paco?")
      No sé; estará en la oficina. ("I don't know; he's probably at the office.")
    - ◆ *¿Dónde estaba Paco?* ("Where was Paco?")
      No sé. Estaría en la oficina. ("I don't know; he was probably at the office.")
  - ▶ Subjunctive
    - ◆ Noun clauses
    - ◆ Adjective clauses
    - ◆ Adverbial clauses
  - ▶ Sequence of tenses

- *No creo que sea interesante.*
- *No me parecía que fuera interesante.*
- *Te daría las direcciones si las supiera.*
▶ Passive voice
  - Used with *ser*
    — *Ese libro fue escrito por un autor conocido.*
  - Impersonal *se* to represent the passive voice
    — *Se abren las puertas a las 9:00.*

■ Word choice
  ▶ Demonstrate the ability to detect, describe, and correct errors in word choice
    - False cognates
      — *asistir; atender*
    - Colloquial expressions and their appropriate use
  ▶ Demonstrate the ability to detect, describe, and correct language that is inappropriate to the task and/or the audience addressed
    - Appropriate register: formal and informal situations

Speech Analysis

For these questions, you will be asked to analyze errors in material recorded by nonnative speakers of Spanish. To successfully complete this task, you must be able to detect, describe, and correct errors in pronunciation, grammar, and word choice.

Writing Analysis

For these questions, you will be asked to analyze errors in writing samples from nonnative writers of Spanish. Answering these questions requires you to use many of the same skills you must use in answering Speech Analysis questions. You may be asked to

■ Demonstrate the ability to detect, describe, or correct basic grammatical errors in written Spanish, as described previously

■ Demonstrate the ability to detect, describe, or correct language that is inappropriate to the task or audience addressed. For example, this could call for the recognition of
  ▶ The misuse of *tú/usted* in various situations
  ▶ The misuse of vocabulary, conveying a meaning that is not intended

Language Analysis

This section will require you to provide explanations for grammatical and word-use errors. Topics in this section may ask you to

■ Demonstrate knowledge of the structural components of the Spanish language. This may include the identification of the correct use of structures such as
  ▶ Direct and indirect objects—their forms and correct placement
  ▶ Placement of adjectives
  ▶ Regular and irregular adjectives
  ▶ The appropriate use of tenses
  ▶ Agreement of nouns and modifiers
  ▶ Subject-verb agreement
  ▶ Idiomatic expressions
  ▶ Comparatives and superlatives

- Demonstrate knowledge of the basic meaningful elements of words
  - ▶ Verb usage
  - ▶ Verbs with spelling changes
  - ▶ Word roots
  - ▶ Prefixes and suffixes

- Demonstrate knowledge of word order to form phrases, clauses, or sentences. This may include
  - ▶ Order of subject and verb in statements versus questions
  - ▶ Order of nouns and modifying adjectives
    - ◆ Adjectives that have different meanings when they precede or follow nouns

- Demonstrate knowledge of the function of cognates and false cognates in the development of vocabulary
  - ▶ Cognates: *doctor* = doctor; *piano* = piano; *silencio* = silence
  - ▶ False cognates: *actual* (means "real" in English, but "current" in Spanish)

- Demonstrate an understanding of the formation of contractions and compound words
  - ▶ *al / del*
  - ▶ *paraguas* (*el paraguas, los paraguas*)

Grammar Analysis

For these questions, you will read sentences in the context of paragraphs from which words or phrases have been omitted. You will be asked to choose the word or phrase that correctly completes the sentence, within the context of the entire paragraph or reading. This part of the test requires knowledge of

- The correct formation and use of regular and irregular verbs in most moods and tenses
  - ▶ Regular and irregular verbs in various tenses
  - ▶ Differentiation between simple past tenses in the indicative (preterite and imperfect)

  - ▶ Use of the subjunctive or the indicative
    - ◆ Sequence of tenses
  - ▶ Use of compound tenses

- The correct formation and use of nouns, adjective, adverbs, and articles
  - ▶ Noun and adjective agreement
  - ▶ Derivation of adverbs
  - ▶ Use of articles
  - ▶ Use of indefinite and negative expressions

- The correct formation and use of pronouns

  - ▶ Use and placement of direct, indirect, and reflexive pronouns
  - ▶ Use and placement of double object pronouns
  - ▶ Use and placement of pronouns with imperatives

- The correct formation and use of conjunctions
  - ▶ *o / u* (when should *u* be used for *o?*); *y / e* (when should *e* be used for *y?*)
  - ▶ When to use conjunctions (join two clauses, in a series, etc.)

Interpretive Reading

Reading selections come from a number of sources, including academic texts; literary selections ranging from classic to contemporary prose and poetry; fiction and nonfiction; media sources such as magazines and newspapers or the Internet; and realia (posters, tickets, advertisements, etc.). The subject matter can be extensive, covering social sciences, cultural topics, humanities, science, education, history, and general interest. Depending on the type, density, and length of the reading selection, it may be followed by one to eight questions. Questions concentrate on content and organization, implied content, language use, main ideas, and supporting details. You should be able to do the following:

- Determine the main idea or purpose of the selection

- Identify other important ideas from the
  - Content and key words
  - Tone of the text
  - Type of language used

- Identify supporting details from the
  - Content and key words

- Identify paraphrases or summaries of ideas from the
  - Content and key words
  - Conclusion of the text

- Identify relationships among ideas directly stated, such as
  - Cause and effect
  - Sequence of ideas
  - Conclusion

- Locate the place in a passage where specific information can be found from
  - Key words
  - The chronology of the text

- Understand a variety of reading materials

You will use the following skills in the reading selection:

- The ability to distinguish what is implied from what is directly stated

- The ability to make inferences from directly stated content

- The ability to recognize the style or manner of expression
  - Literary
  - Narrative
  - Informational
  - Persuasive

- The ability to distinguish fact from opinion

You will need to be able to recognize how the meaning of a word, sentence, or paragraph is affected by the context in which it appears. You may also need to determine the meaning of figurative language. It is important to understand the function of key transition indicators, such as *sin embargo, no obstante, con todo, por eso*.

The following exercise and annotated sample are intended to give you practice using the kinds of interpretive thinking that are expected in this section of the test. Although the format of the annotation exercise is not like that of the multiple-choice questions on the test, the types and levels of understanding and evaluation needed to complete it are comparable. Read the passage and try to annotate key words, phrases, and sentences in the passage. Then, read the annotated version on the following pages and compare your analysis. Finally, examine the multiple-choice questions that follow the annotated version to see how the skills you use in annotating the passage will be applied on the test.

Asistí durante un otoño a la escuela de la Srta. Leocadia en la aldea, porque mi salud no andaba bien y el abuelo retrasó mi vuelta a la ciudad. Como era el tiempo frío y estaban los suelos embarrados, y no se veía rastro de muchachos, me aburría dentro de la casa y le pedí al abuelo asisitir a la escuela. El abuelo consintió y acudí a aquella casita alargada y blanca de cal, con el tejado pajizo y requemado por el sol y las nieves, en las afueras del pueblo.

La Srta. Leocadia era alta y gruesa; tenía el carácter más bien áspero y grandes juanetes en los pies que la obligaban a andar como quien arrastra cadenas. Las clases en la escuela, con la lluvia rebotando en el tejado y en los cristales, con las moscas pegajosas de la tormenta persiguiéndose alrededor de la bombilla, tenían su atractivo. Recuerdo especialmente a un muchacho de unos diez años, hijo de un aparcero muy pobre, llamado Ivo. Era un muchacho delgado, de ojos azules, que bizqueaba ligeramente al hablar. Todos los muchachos y muchachas de la escuela admiraban y envidiaban un poco a Ivo, por el don que poseía de atraer la atención sobre sí en todo momento. No es que fuera ni inteligente ni gracioso y, sin embargo, había algo en él, en su voz quizás, en las cosas que contaba, que conseguía cautivar a quien le escuchase. También la Srta. Leocadia se dejaba prender de aquella red de plata que Ivo tendía a cuantos atendían sus enrevesadas conversaciones, y—yo creo que muchas veces contra su voluntad—la Srta. Leocadia le confiaba a Ivo tareas deseadas por todos o distinciones que merecían alumnos más estudiosos y aplicados.

Quizás lo que más se envidiaba de Ivo era la posesión de la codiciada llave de la torrecita. Esta era, en efecto, una pequeña torre situada en un ángulo de la escuela, en cuyo interior se guardaban los libros de lectura. Allí entraba Ivo a buscarlos y allí volvía a dejarlos, al terminar la clase. La Srta. Leocadia se lo encomendó a él, nadie sabía en realidad por qué.

Ivo estaba muy orgulloso de esta distinción y por nada del mundo la hubiera cedido. Un día, Mateo Heredia, el más aplicado y estudioso de la escuela, pidió encargarse de la tarea—a todos nos fascinaba el misterioso interior de la torrecita, donde no entramos nunca—y la Srta. Leocadia pareció acceder. Pero Ivo se levantó y, acercándose a la maestra, empezó a hablarle en su voz baja, bizqueando los ojos y moviendo mucho las manos, como tenía por costumbre. La maestra dudó un poco, y al fin dijo:

—Quede todo como estaba. Que siga encargándose Ivo de la torrecita.

Now compare your annotations with the ones below.

> The descriptions indicate a rural setting. We see that the narrator suffered from poor health as a child.

The weather, combined with poor health, caused the narrator to have to remain indoors; he wanted to go to school to avoid boredom.

Asistí durante un otoño a la escuela de la Srta. Leocadia en la aldea, porque mi salud no andaba bien y el abuelo retrasó mi vuelta a la ciudad. Como era el tiempo frío y estaban los suelos embarrados, y no se veía rastro de muchachos, me aburría dentro de la casa y le pedí al abuelo asisitir a la escuela. El abuelo consintió y acudí a aquella casita alargada y blanca de cal, con el tejado pajizo y requemado por el sol y las nieves, en las afueras del pueblo.

La Srta. Leocadia era alta y gruesa; tenía el carácter más bien áspero y grandes juanetes en los pies que la obligaban a andar como quien arrastra cadenas. Las clases en la escuela, con la lluvia rebotando en el tejado y en los cristales, con las moscas pegajosas de la tormenta persiguiéndose alrededor de la bombilla, tenían su atractivo. Recuerdo especialmente a un muchacho de unos diez años, hijo de un aparcero muy pobre, llamado Ivo. Era un muchacho delgado, de ojos azules, que bizqueaba ligeramente al hablar. Todos los muchachos y muchachas de la escuela admiraban y envidiaban un poco a Ivo, por el don que poseía de atraer la atención sobre sí en todo momento. No es que fuera ni inteligente ni gracioso y, sin embargo, había algo en él, en su voz quizás, en las cosas que contaba, que conseguía cautivar a quien le escuchase. También la Srta. Leocadia se dejaba prender de aquella red de plata que Ivo tendía a cuantos atendían sus enrevesadas conversaciones, y—yo creo que muchas veces contra su voluntad—la Srta. Leocadia le confiaba a Ivo tareas deseadas por todos o distinciones que merecían alumnos más estudiosos y aplicados.

Consider the use of the word *don* here (refers to his "talent" for attracting attention).

Further description of how Ivo captures others' attention.

Teacher's reaction to Ivo.

> The use of words such as *gruesa, carácter . . . áspero, como quien arrastra cadenas* convey the description of a somewhat pathetic person.

> Description of Ivo, as well as other classmates' descriptions of him.

> This part highlights a description of Ivo by contrast *(no es que fuera ni inteligente ni gracioso; distinciones que merecían alumnos más estudiosos)*.

Why else Ivo was envied.

Consider what the key and the *torrecita* might represent.

Quizás lo que más se envidiaba de Ivo era la posesión de la codiciada llave de la torrecita. Esta era, en efecto, una pequeña torre situada en un ángulo de la escuela, en cuyo interior se guardaban los libros de lectura. Allí entraba Ivo a buscarlos y allí volvía a dejarlos, al terminar la clase. La Srta. Leocadia se lo encomendó a él, nadie sabía en realidad por qué.

There is a certain mystery to the key and the tower full of books. Only Ivo has the key and can enter the tower.

Description of how pleased Ivo is with his job.

Ivo estaba muy orgulloso de esta distinción y por nada del mundo la hubiera cedido. Un día, Mateo Heredia, el más aplicado y estudioso de la escuela, pidió encargarse de la tarea—a todos nos fascinaba el misterioso interior de la torrecita, donde no entramos nunca—y la Srta. Leocadia pareció acceder. Pero Ivo se levantó y, acercándose a la maestra, empezó a hablarle en su voz baja, bizqueando los ojos y moviendo mucho las manos, como tenía por costumbre. La maestra dudó un poco, y al fin dijo:

Another student asks for the job, but Ivo defends his dominance.

Crossing his eyes and moving his hands indicate Ivo's nervous nature.

—Quede todo como estaba. Que siga encargándose Ivo de la torrecita.

Following a nervous but quiet plea, the teacher agrees that Ivo will remain in charge of the tower.

Here are some possible multiple-choice questions that address the reading passage on the previous page:

¿Por qué está el narrador en el pueblo en el otoño?

  (A)   Para visitar a su abuelo
  (B)   Para asistir a la escuela con sus amigos
  (C)   Porque es amigo de la Srta. Leocadia
  (D)   Porque su salud lo requiere

Choice (D) is the correct answer. All choices are mentioned in the passage, but only (D) is a cause mentioned in the reading.

Se describe a la Srta. Leocadia como una mujer

  (A)   graciosa
  (B)   talentosa
  (C)   poco atractiva
  (D)   muy estudiosa

Choice (C) is the correct answer. The descriptions in choices (A), (B), and (D) are alluded to with regard to other characters, but those that refer to Srta. Leocadia clearly support choice (C).

¿Qué sienten los compañeros de Ivo hacia él?

  (A)   Lo compadecen.
  (B)   Le tienen envidia.
  (C)   Les parece ridículo.
  (D)   Están orgullosos de él.

Choice (B) is the correct answer. Choices (A) and (C) might reflect likely childhood behavior; choice (D) might be chosen if the passage is misread; choice (B) is the reaction actually mentioned in the passage.

¿Cuál de las siguientes palabras refleja el ambiente que describe el autor?

  (A)   Misterioso
  (B)   Alegre
  (C)   Arriesgado
  (D)   Sombrío

Choice (A) is the correct answer. There are many "mysteries" to the passage: What is the nature of the author's illness? Why does the teacher give Ivo a prized task? What does Ivo whisper to the teacher?

¿Por qué quieren los muchachos de la escuela que la llave de la torrecita pase a otra persona?

  (A)   Para poder ir allí con más frecuencia
  (B)   Para poder leer los libros que había allí
  (C)   Para quitarle la distinción a Ivo
  (D)   Para saber qué secretos encerraba la torre

Choice (D) is the correct answer. While this is an inference question, the clue is clearly offered in the last paragraph.

Cultural Perspectives

Questions in the Cultural Perspectives section focus on the following areas: geography, lifestyles and societies, sociolinguistic elements of the Spanish-speaking world, history, and literature and the arts. The following is a suggested list of possible topics that may appear in the Cultural Perspectives section. This list is in no way comprehensive, but it provides an idea of the type of topics related to Hispanic culture that may appear in the test.

Geography

- Locating Spanish-speaking regions, countries, and capitals in
  - Europe
  - North America
  - Central America and the Caribbean
  - South America
  - Spanish-speaking areas within the United States

- Identifying major geographical features of Spanish-speaking regions and countries, such as
  - Climate and seasons
    - Opposite seasons in Northern and Southern Hemispheres
  - Agricultural features, natural resources, exports
  - Landmarks (e.g., Chichén Itzá, Nazca, Lake Titicaca, Iguazú Falls)
  - Rivers, mountain areas, borders

Lifestyles and Societies

- Food and mealtimes
  - Traditional dishes
  - Regional dishes
  - Food and beverages important to cultural traditions

- Customs
  - Salutations
  - Register
  - Monetary units
  - Family events (e.g., *quinceañeras*)
  - Surnames
  - Expression of times of day, weeks (calendars usually begin with Monday)
  - Expression of dates
  - Extended family units

- Holidays
  - *Año Nuevo*
  - *El Día de los Reyes*
  - *Carnaval*
  - *Semana Santa*
  - *El Día de los Muertos*
  - *Las Fallas*
  - *La Tomatina*
  - *Cinco de Mayo*
  - *Los Sanfermines*
  - *Navidades*
  - *Nochebuena*

- Regional variations
  - Food
  - Languages
  - Schedules

- Foreign influences
  - Bordering nations
  - Language influences

Sociolinguistic Elements of Spanish

- Social interaction patterns
  - Greetings and goodbyes
  - Introductions

- Language appropriate to task and audiences
  - Situationally appropriate discourse
  - Conversational transitions

- Idiomatic expressions, common sayings, proverbs
  - *Me estás tomando el pelo.* ("You're pulling my leg.")
  - *Hay que dejarle tiempo al tiempo.* ("You have to let time take its course.")
  - *Más vale pájaro en mano que cien volando.* ("A bird in the hand is worth two in the bush.")

History

- Key eras
  - Pre-Columbian civilizations in the western hemisphere
    - Toltec, Maya, Inca, Aztec, Chibcha, Guaraní
  - Early civilizations in the Iberian peninsula
  - Jewish, Moorish, and Christian civilizations in Iberia/Spain
  - Exploration of the "New World"
    - Columbus, Cortés, Pizarro, Ponce de León
  - Colonization and expansion in the Western Hemisphere
  - Notable monarchs and other figures in Spain
    - The Catholic Monarchs
  - Independence movements of Spanish America
    - Notable figures
      - Bolívar
      - San Martín
      - Martí
    - The Mexican Revolution and its reforms
      - Benito Juárez
      - Pancho Villa
      - Father Hidalgo
  - United States intervention
    - The Spanish-American War

- Current events in Spanish America
  - Farm workers in the United States
    - César Chávez
  - Revolution and change
    - Juan Perón
    - Salvador Allende
    - Fulgencio Batista
    - Violeta Chamorro
    - Fidel Castro
    - Che Guevara
    - Óscar Arias
  - Current events in Spain
    - Notable figures and transitions
      - The Spanish Civil War
      - Francisco Franco
      - Juan Carlos I
  - Contributions of Spanish language/culture to other cultures
    - English words derived from Spanish
    - Spanish words derived from English
  - Basic economic and trade factors
    - Currencies
    - Vocabulary
    - The Panama Canal
    - Tourism

Literature and the Arts

- Major works and authors of the literature of Spain, Spanish America, and Spanish or bilingual writers in the United States. For example,
  - *El cantar de Mío Cid*
  - *El libro de buen amor*
  - *La Araucana*
  - *La Celestina*
  - *Don Quijote de La Mancha*
  - *Sor Juana Inés de la Cruz*
  - *Literatura picaresca*
  - *Literatura del Siglo de Oro*
  - *Literatura gauchesca*
  - Gustavo Adolfo Bécquer

- ► *La Generación del '98*
- ► Federico García Lorca
- ► *El realismo mágico*
- ► Gabriel García Márquez
- ► Isabel Allende
- ► Esmeralda Santiago

■ Significant figures, works, and events in the arts
  - ► Pre-Columbian art and architecture
    - ◆ *Isla de Pascua*
    - ◆ *Líneas de Nazca*
    - ◆ *Machu Picchu*
    - ◆ *Teotihuacán*
    - ◆ *Tulúm*
    - ◆ *Uzmal*
  - ► Early art in the Iberian Peninsula
    - ◆ *Las Cuevas de Altamira*
    - ◆ Roman architecture
    - ◆ Moorish architecture
      - — *La Alhambra*
      - — *La mezquita de Córdoba*
  - ► Art and architecture of Spanish America
    - ◆ Colonial art and architecture
    - ◆ The muralist movement
      - — Rivera
      - — Orozco
      - — Siqueiros
    - ◆ Kahlo
    - ◆ Botero
  - ► Art and architecture of Spain
    - ◆ El Greco
    - ◆ Velázquez
    - ◆ Goya
    - ◆ Picasso
    - ◆ Miró
    - ◆ Dalí
    - ◆ Gaudí

- ► Music and musicians
  - ◆ *Pasodoble*
  - ◆ *Tango*
  - ◆ *Salsa*
  - ◆ *Flamenco*
  - ◆ *Zarzuelas*
  - ◆ Andrés Segovia
  - ◆ Pablo Casals
  - ◆ Celia Cruz
  - ◆ Isaac Albéniz
  - ◆ Plácido Domingo
- ► Theater
  - ◆ Calderón de la Barca
  - ◆ Lope de Vega
  - ◆ Tirso de Molina
  - ◆ *Los corrales*
  - ◆ García Lorca
  - ◆ *Teatro campesino*
- ► Museums
  - ◆ *El Prado* in Madrid
  - ◆ Guggenheim Museum in Bilbao
  - ◆ *El Museo del Barrio* in New York

Once again, test takers are reminded that this is not an all-inclusive list; nor will these specific examples appear on every test. These are simply areas, topics, events, and figures that represent the major categories that are covered: geography, lifestyles and societies, sociolinguistic elements, history, and literature and the arts.

Chapter 4
Succeeding on Multiple-Choice Questions

▶ ▶ ▶ ▶ ▶ ▶ ▶ ▶ ▶ ▶ ▶ ▶ ▶

Understanding Multiple-Choice Questions

When you read multiple-choice questions on the Praxis *Spanish: Content Knowledge* test, you will probably notice that the syntax (word order) is different from the word order you're used to seeing in ordinary material that you read, such as newspapers or textbooks. One of the reasons for this difference is that many test questions contain the phrase "which of the following."

To answer a multiple-choice question successfully, you need to consider carefully the context set up by the question and limit your choice of answers to the list given. The purpose of the phrase "which of the following" is to remind you to do this. For example, look at this question.

> Which of the following is a flavor made from beans?
>
> (A) Strawberry
> (B) Cherry
> (C) Vanilla
> (D) Mint

You may know that chocolate and coffee are also flavors made from beans, but they are not listed, and the question asks you to select from the list that follows ("which of the following"). So the answer has to be the only bean-derived flavor in the list: vanilla.

Notice that the answer can be substituted for the phrase "which of the following." In the question above, you could insert "vanilla" for "which of the following" and have the sentence "Vanilla is a flavor made from beans." Sometimes it helps to cross out "which of the following" and insert the various choices. You may want to give this technique a try as you answer various multiple-choice practice questions.

Looking carefully at the "which of the following" phrase helps you to focus on what the question is asking you to find and on the answer choices. In the simple example above, all of the answer choices are flavors. Your job is to decide which of the flavors is the one made from beans.

The vanilla bean question is straightforward. But the phrase "which of the following" can also be found in more challenging questions. Look at this question:

> ¿Cuál de los siguientes personajes se asocia con el movimiento de independencia
> de la Argentina del siglo XIX?
>
> (A) Porfirio Díaz
> (B) Simón Bolívar
> (C) Fulgencio Batista
> (D) José de San Martín

The placement of "¿cuál de los siguientes?" ("which of the following") tells you that the list of choices consists of several people. What are you supposed to find as an answer? You are supposed to identify the person who is linked to the movement for Argentinian independence in the nineteenth century.

ETS question writers and editors work very hard to word each question as clearly as possible. Sometimes, though, it helps to put the question in your own words. Here, you could paraphrase the question as "Which person helped to make Argentina independent?" The correct answer is (D).

You may also find that it helps you to circle or underline each of the critical details of the question in your test book so you don't miss any of them. It's only by looking at all parts of the question carefully that you will have all of the information you need to answer it. Circle or underline the critical parts of what is being asked in this question.

Which of the following is a noun suffix that indicates a place where business or work is performed?
(A) *-ero*
(B) *-istas*
(C) *-ismo*
(D) *-ería*

Here is one possible way you may have annotated the question:

Which of the following is a <u>noun suffix</u> that indicates a place where business or work is performed?
(A) *-ero*
(B) *-istas*
(C) *-ismo*
(D) *-ería*

After thinking about the question, you can probably see that you are being given four noun suffixes and are being asked to identify which one is used for businesses or workplaces. The correct answer is (D). The important thing is understanding what the question is asking. With enough practice, you should be able to determine what any question is asking. Knowing the answer is, of course, a different matter, but you have to understand a question before you can answer it correctly.

Understanding Questions Containing NOT, LEAST, or EXCEPT

The words "NOT," "LEAST," and "EXCEPT" can make comprehension of test questions more difficult. They ask you to select the choice that *doesn't* fit. You must be very careful with this question type because it's easy to forget that you're selecting the negative. This question type is used in situations in which there are several good solutions, or ways to approach something, but also a clearly wrong way. These words are always capitalized when they appear in The Praxis Series test questions, but they are easily (and frequently) overlooked.

For the following test question, determine what kind of answer you need and what the details of the question are.

Un crucero por el Mar Caribe haría escala en los siguientes puertos EXCEPTO

(A) San Juan, Puerto Rico
(B) Santo Domingo
(C) Cozumel
(D) Palma de Mallorca

You're looking for a seaport that is NOT on the Caribbean Sea. (D) is the correct answer. Palma de Mallorca is on the Mediterranean Sea.

TIP

It's easy to get confused while you're processing the information to answer a question that contains a "NOT," "LEAST," or "EXCEPT." If you treat the word "NOT" as one of the details you must satisfy, you have a better chance of understanding what the question is asking. And when you check your answer, make "NOT" one of the details you check for.

Be Familiar with Question Types Based on Recorded Excerpts

The first two sections of the *Spanish: Content Knowledge* test will require you to listen to spoken Spanish that is recorded on CD. The CD will be played **only once**. Although some of the recorded material will be printed in the test book, some will not, so it is important that you listen carefully to the spoken material. The questions based on the recorded material will be in several formats.

1. Interpretive Listening—Short Conversations

In this type of question, you listen to a recording of native Spanish speakers conversing at a normal conversational rate of speed. You then are asked one or more questions based on what you have heard. Neither the dialogue nor the questions are printed in your test book. In the following example, a narrator introduces the following dialogue:

(Narrator) *Un señor pide ayuda.*

(Man) *A ver si me puede ayudar, señorita. Quiero hacer una llamada de larga distancia a Bogotá.*

(Woman) *Cómo no. Primero tiene que marcar el número internacional, cero-uno-uno y luego el código cincuenta y siete de Colombia. Para Bogotá, el código es el número 1. Luego marque el número de la persona.*

(Narrator) *¿Con quién está hablando el hombre?*

Then, in your test book you see the following choices:

(A) Con la oficina de turismo.
(B) Con la operadora de teléfono.
(C) Con un agente de viajes.
(D) Con el ayuntamiento de Bogotá.

To answer, you must select the choice that best answers the narrator's question: with whom is the man speaking? The correct answer is (B), because it is evident from the context that the man is talking to a telephone operator.

2. Interpretive Listening—Short Narrations

This question type is similar to the one discussed in the previous section, except that instead of a conversation you hear a short narration. The narration is not printed in your test book. After each narration, you will hear one or more questions, which are printed in your test book. You may find it useful to take notes in your test book as you listen to the narration.

Here is an example, introduced by the narrator:

(Narrator) *Esta pregunta se refiere a un anuncio en la radio.*

(Man) *¡Señoras y señores! ¡Aprovechen esta oferta inicial! Durante el mes de marzo únicamente estaremos ofreciendo precios especiales en nuestras instalaciones recién construidas, con sabor antiguo. Recámaras a todo lujo, servicio completo veinticuatro horas al día, con piscina cubierta, gimnasio y dos restaurantes fabulosos. ¡Hagan sus reservaciones antes del quince de febrero y reciban un bono especial!*

Then, in your test book you see the following question and answer choices:

¿De qué se habla en el anuncio?

- (A)   De un viaje.
- (B)   De un concurso.
- (C)   De una tienda.
- (D)   De un hotel.

The correct answer is (D), because the announcement refers to hotel facilities.

3. Interpretive Listening—Long Conversations and Narrations

These formats are the same as those discussed in the previous two sections, except that the narrative passage or conversation is longer. After each narration or conversation, you will hear several questions which are printed in your test book.

4. Questions about Structure of the Language Based on Recorded Excerpts

Section II of the *Spanish: Content Knowledge* test is called Structure of the Language (Grammatical Accuracy) and includes both listening and reading selections.

In the first part of section II, you hear recorded selections spoken by students who are learning Spanish and who make errors in their speech. Their words are not printed in your test book. The following example begins with the voice of the narrator:

(Narrator)   *Question 4 refers to the following greetings.*

(Student)   *¡Hola, Andrea! Hace mucho tiempo que no te vea. ¿Cómo estás?*

(Narrator)   *Question Number 4: Identify the error in the excerpt.*

You hear again:

(Student)   *Hace mucho tiempo que no te vea.*

In your test book you read the following:

Question 4 refers to the following greetings.

4. Identify the grammatical error in the excerpt.

- (A)   *Hace*
- (B)   *tiempo*
- (C)   *te*
- (D)   *vea*

The correct answer is (D), because the speaker should have used the indicative mood (e.g., "*veo*") and not the subjunctive ("*vea*").

Be Familiar with Question Types Based on Written Excerpts

1. Questions about Structure of the Language Based on Written Excerpts

In the second part of Section II, you read paragraphs written by students who are learning Spanish. The student writing contains errors, and your task is to identify, correct, or describe the type of error made in a particular sentence from the paragraph. Each sentence selected contains only <u>one</u> error. When you answer the question, it helps to consider the meaning of the sentence and the type of error in the context of the whole paragraph. You may find it useful to take notes in your test book.

Here is an example:

This question refers to the following note left for a friend.

(1) *¡Apúrate, Juan!* (2) *Deje el trabajo para más tarde. ¡Acuérdate!* (3) *La última vez que fuimos, no cabimos en el auditorio.* (4) *Todos los asientos estaban ocupadas.*

Identify the error in sentence 2.

(A) *Deje*
(B) *el trabajo*
(C) *para*
(D) *más tarde*

The correct answer is (A), because given the context of the text and in particular the initial use of the informal command, the consistent use of the informal is required (in this case, *Deja* instead of *Deje*).

2. Fill-in-the-blank questions

Some questions in Section II feature Spanish sentences or paragraphs in which words or phrases have been removed and replaced with a blank space. You are presented with four options for filling in the blank. Your task is to choose the option that results in the best sentence or paragraph in written Spanish. Here is an example:

¡Qué suerte tuvimos! Compramos el carro nuevo por menos _____ pensábamos.

(A) de que
(B) de lo que
(C) de
(D) del que

The correct answer is (B), because comparison of a whole idea followed by an inflected verb is expressed by *de lo que*.

3. Interpretive Reading questions

In Section III of the *Spanish: Content Knowledge* test, you read several selections in Spanish. Each selection is followed by one or more questions. Your task is to answer each question based only on what is stated or implied in the selection. You may find it helpful to take notes in your test book.

Here is an example:

Esta pregunta se refiere al pasaje siguiente.

Línea   La historia de la astronomía está íntimamente vinculada con la de la fotografía. Después de milenios de estudiar el cielo a simple vista y siglos de hacerlo con el telescopio, los astrónomos comenzaron a valerse de la placa fotográfica durante el siglo XIX.

       Las primeras aplicaciones de la fotografía en la astronomía se remontan al año 1839. A partir de
(5) entonces, muchos de los grandes descubrimientos astronómicos se realizaron con la ayuda de la placa fotográfica.

       La astronomía mexicana comenzó a utilizar muy pronto la fotografía. En 1874, después de una expedición casi heroica, una comisión mexicana, encabezada por don Francisco Díaz Covarrubias, llegó al Japón para fotografiar el tránsito de Venus por el disco solar. Dicha misión cumplió exitosamente su
(10) cometido y publicó sus resultados en 1875, antes que los otros grupos de diversos países que también habían ido a fotografiar el evento.

      ¿Cuál es la idea central de este pasaje?

    (A)   Los inicios de la astronomía en Japón y su impacto en México
    (B)   Los descubrimientos astronómicos del siglo XIX
    (C)   La interacción entre la fotografía y la astronomia en el siglo XIX
    (D)   El reemplazo de las placas fotográficas por los telescopios de hoy en día

You are being asked to identify the main idea of the passage. The correct answer is (C). In line 1, and throughout the passage, reference is made to the important role photography has had in the development of astronomy.

Other Formats

New formats are developed from time to time to find new ways of assessing knowledge with multiple-choice questions. If you see a format you are not familiar with, read the directions carefully. Then read and approach the question the way you would any other question, asking yourself what you are supposed to be looking for and what details are given in the question that help you find the answer.

Other Useful Facts about the Test

1. **You can answer the questions that do not require listening in any order.** You can go through the questions with written prompts from beginning to end, as many test takers do, or you can create your own path. Perhaps you will want to answer questions in your strongest area of knowledge first and then move from your strengths to your weaker areas. There is no right or wrong way. Use the approach that works best for you.

   You do not have this liberty with the questions that require you to listen to a recording. You must answer those questions in the order in which you hear them and in the time that the recording permits. You are not allowed to pause the recording for extra time.

2. **There are no trick questions on the test.** You don't have to find any hidden meanings or worry about trick wording. All of the questions on the test ask about subject matter knowledge in a straightforward manner.

3. **Don't worry about answer patterns.** There is one myth that says that answers on multiple-choice tests follow patterns. Another myth says that there will never be more than two questions with the same lettered answer following each other. There is no truth to either of these myths. Select the answer you think is correct based on your knowledge of the subject.

4. **There is no penalty for guessing.** Your test score for multiple-choice questions is based on the number of correct answers you have. When you don't know the answer to a question, try to eliminate any obviously wrong answers and then guess at the correct one.

5. **It's OK to write in your test book.** You can work out problems right on the pages of the book, make notes to yourself, mark questions you want to review later, or write anything at all. Your test book will be destroyed after you are finished with it, so use it in any way that is helpful to you. But make sure to mark your answers on the answer sheet.

Smart Tips for Taking the Test

1. **Put your answers in the right "bubbles."** It seems obvious, but be sure that you are filling in the answer bubble that corresponds to the question you are answering. A significant number of test takers fill in a bubble without checking to see that the number matches the question they are answering.

2. **Skip the nonlistening questions you find extremely difficult.** In the section of the test that does not require listening to a recording, there are sure to be some questions that you think are hard. Rather than trying to answer these on your first pass through this part of the test, leave them blank and mark them in your test booklet so that you can come back to them later. Pay attention to the time as you answer the rest of the questions on the test, and try to finish with 10 or 15 minutes remaining so that you can go back over the questions you left blank. Even if you don't know the answer the second time you read the questions, see if you can narrow down the possible answers, and then guess.

3. **Keep track of the time.** In the part of the test that requires you to listen to a recording, you must answer within a specific period of time. For the rest of the test, however, you will need to budget your time for yourself. Bring a watch to the test, just in case the clock in the test room is difficult for you to see. You will probably have plenty of time to answer all of the questions, but if you find yourself becoming bogged down in one section, you might decide to move on and come back to that section later.

4. **Read all of the possible answers before selecting one**—and then reread the question to be sure the answer you have selected really answers the question being asked. Remember that a question that contains a phrase such as "which of the following does NOT ..." is asking for the one answer that is NOT a correct statement or conclusion.

5. **Check your answers.** If you have extra time left over at the end of the test, look over each question and make sure that you have filled in the bubble on the answer sheet as you intended. Many test takers make careless mistakes that they could have corrected if they had checked their answers.

6. **Don't worry about your score when you are taking the test.** No one is expected to answer all of the questions correctly. Your score on this test is not analogous to your score on the SAT, the GRE, or other similar-looking (but in fact very different!) tests. It doesn't matter on this test whether you score very high or barely pass. If you meet the minimum passing scores for your state and you meet the state's other requirements for obtaining a teaching license, you will receive a license. In other words, your actual score doesn't matter, as long as it is above the minimum required score. With your score report you will receive a booklet entitled *Understanding Your Praxis Scores*, which lists the passing scores for your state.

Chapter 5
Practice Questions—*Spanish: Content Knowledge*

▶   ▶   ▶   ▶   ▶   ▶   ▶   ▶   ▶   ▶   ▶   ▶

Now that you have studied the content topics and have worked through strategies relating to multiple-choice questions, you should answer the following practice questions. You will probably find it helpful to simulate actual testing conditions, giving yourself 90 minutes to work on the questions. You can cut out and use the answer sheet provided if you wish.

When you have finished the practice questions, you can score your answers and read the explanations for the best answer choices in chapter 6.

The listening section for this practice test is found on the Spanish CD included with this study guide. Tracks 1-5 refer to the *Spanish: Content Knowledge* test. (Note that tracks 6-13 refer to the *Spanish: Productive Language Skills* test; you will not need to listen to this section of the CD unless you are planning to take that test as well.) As you listen to the CD, you will notice that pauses have been included in the narration. During the pauses, you may bubble in your answers on the provided answer sheet.

To simulate actual testing conditions, do not stop your CD player during the practice test.

Keep in mind that the test you take at an actual administration will have different questions, although the proportion of questions in each area and major subarea will be approximately the same. You should not expect the percentage of questions you answer correctly on this practice test to be exactly the same as when you take the test at an actual administration, because numerous factors affect a person's performance in any given testing situation.

THE **PRAXIS**
S E R I E S
Professional Assessments for Beginning Teachers ®

TEST NAME:

Spanish: Content Knowledge (0191)
Practice Questions

Time—90 Minutes

90 Questions

**(Note: At the official test administration, there will be 120 questions,
and you will be allowed 120 minutes to complete the test.)**

DO NOT USE INK

Use only a pencil with soft black lead (No. 2 or HB) to complete this answer sheet.
Be sure to fill in completely the oval that corresponds to the proper letter or number.
Completely erase any errors or stray marks.

(ETS) THE PRAXIS SERIES
Professional Assessments for Beginning Teachers

Answer Sheet L

1. NAME
Enter your last name and first initial.
Omit spaces, hyphens, apostrophes, etc.

Last Name (first 6 letters) — F I

A B C D E F G H I J K L M N O P Q R S T U V W X Y Z

2.

YOUR NAME: (Print)
Last Name (Family or Surname) — First Name (Given) — M. I.

MAILING ADDRESS: (Print)
P.O. Box or Street Address — Apt. # (If any)
City — State or Province
Country — Zip or Postal Code

TELEPHONE NUMBER: Home — Business

SIGNATURE: — **TEST DATE:**

3. DATE OF BIRTH
Month — Day

Jan. Feb. Mar. April May June July Aug. Sept. Oct. Nov. Dec.

0 1 2 3 4 5 6 7 8 9

4. SOCIAL SECURITY NUMBER

0 1 2 3 4 5 6 7 8 9

5. CANDIDATE ID NUMBER

0 1 2 3 4 5 6 7 8 9

6. TEST CENTER / REPORTING LOCATION

Center Number — Room Number
Center Name
City — State or Province
Country

7. TEST CODE / FORM CODE

0 1 2 3 4 5 6 7 8 9

8. TEST BOOK SERIAL NUMBER

9. TEST FORM
0
1

10. TEST NAME

Educational Testing Service, ETS, the ETS logo and THE PRAXIS SERIES: PROFESSIONAL ASSESSMENTS FOR BEGINNING TEACHERS are registered trademarks of Educational Testing Service. The Praxis Series is a trademark of Educational Testing Service.

Copyright © 2004 by Educational Testing Service, Princeton, NJ 08541-0001. All rights reserved. Printed in U.S.A.

51055 • 14725 • TF24E50 • printed in U.S.A.
MH04023   I.N. 202984   Q3032-06,07

1   2   3   4

8

CERTIFICATION STATEMENT: (Please write the following statement below. DO NOT PRINT.)
"I hereby agree to the conditions set forth in the Registration Bulletin and certify that I am the person whose name and address appear on this answer sheet."

_____

_____

_____

SIGNATURE: _____   DATE: _____ / _____ / _____
                                                          Month   Day   Year

BE SURE EACH MARK IS DARK AND COMPLETELY FILLS THE INTENDED SPACE AS ILLUSTRATED HERE: ● .

1–30	31–60	61–90	91–120
1 Ⓐ Ⓑ Ⓒ Ⓓ	31 Ⓐ Ⓑ Ⓒ Ⓓ	61 Ⓐ Ⓑ Ⓒ Ⓓ	91 Ⓐ Ⓑ Ⓒ Ⓓ
2 Ⓐ Ⓑ Ⓒ Ⓓ	32 Ⓐ Ⓑ Ⓒ Ⓓ	62 Ⓐ Ⓑ Ⓒ Ⓓ	92 Ⓐ Ⓑ Ⓒ Ⓓ
3 Ⓐ Ⓑ Ⓒ Ⓓ	33 Ⓐ Ⓑ Ⓒ Ⓓ	63 Ⓐ Ⓑ Ⓒ Ⓓ	93 Ⓐ Ⓑ Ⓒ Ⓓ
4 Ⓐ Ⓑ Ⓒ Ⓓ	34 Ⓐ Ⓑ Ⓒ Ⓓ	64 Ⓐ Ⓑ Ⓒ Ⓓ	94 Ⓐ Ⓑ Ⓒ Ⓓ
5 Ⓐ Ⓑ Ⓒ Ⓓ	35 Ⓐ Ⓑ Ⓒ Ⓓ	65 Ⓐ Ⓑ Ⓒ Ⓓ	95 Ⓐ Ⓑ Ⓒ Ⓓ
6 Ⓐ Ⓑ Ⓒ Ⓓ	36 Ⓐ Ⓑ Ⓒ Ⓓ	66 Ⓐ Ⓑ Ⓒ Ⓓ	96 Ⓐ Ⓑ Ⓒ Ⓓ
7 Ⓐ Ⓑ Ⓒ Ⓓ	37 Ⓐ Ⓑ Ⓒ Ⓓ	67 Ⓐ Ⓑ Ⓒ Ⓓ	97 Ⓐ Ⓑ Ⓒ Ⓓ
8 Ⓐ Ⓑ Ⓒ Ⓓ	38 Ⓐ Ⓑ Ⓒ Ⓓ	68 Ⓐ Ⓑ Ⓒ Ⓓ	98 Ⓐ Ⓑ Ⓒ Ⓓ
9 Ⓐ Ⓑ Ⓒ Ⓓ	39 Ⓐ Ⓑ Ⓒ Ⓓ	69 Ⓐ Ⓑ Ⓒ Ⓓ	99 Ⓐ Ⓑ Ⓒ Ⓓ
10 Ⓐ Ⓑ Ⓒ Ⓓ	40 Ⓐ Ⓑ Ⓒ Ⓓ	70 Ⓐ Ⓑ Ⓒ Ⓓ	100 Ⓐ Ⓑ Ⓒ Ⓓ
11 Ⓐ Ⓑ Ⓒ Ⓓ	41 Ⓐ Ⓑ Ⓒ Ⓓ	71 Ⓐ Ⓑ Ⓒ Ⓓ	101 Ⓐ Ⓑ Ⓒ Ⓓ
12 Ⓐ Ⓑ Ⓒ Ⓓ	42 Ⓐ Ⓑ Ⓒ Ⓓ	72 Ⓐ Ⓑ Ⓒ Ⓓ	102 Ⓐ Ⓑ Ⓒ Ⓓ
13 Ⓐ Ⓑ Ⓒ Ⓓ	43 Ⓐ Ⓑ Ⓒ Ⓓ	73 Ⓐ Ⓑ Ⓒ Ⓓ	103 Ⓐ Ⓑ Ⓒ Ⓓ
14 Ⓐ Ⓑ Ⓒ Ⓓ	44 Ⓐ Ⓑ Ⓒ Ⓓ	74 Ⓐ Ⓑ Ⓒ Ⓓ	104 Ⓐ Ⓑ Ⓒ Ⓓ
15 Ⓐ Ⓑ Ⓒ Ⓓ	45 Ⓐ Ⓑ Ⓒ Ⓓ	75 Ⓐ Ⓑ Ⓒ Ⓓ	105 Ⓐ Ⓑ Ⓒ Ⓓ
16 Ⓐ Ⓑ Ⓒ Ⓓ	46 Ⓐ Ⓑ Ⓒ Ⓓ	76 Ⓐ Ⓑ Ⓒ Ⓓ	106 Ⓐ Ⓑ Ⓒ Ⓓ
17 Ⓐ Ⓑ Ⓒ Ⓓ	47 Ⓐ Ⓑ Ⓒ Ⓓ	77 Ⓐ Ⓑ Ⓒ Ⓓ	107 Ⓐ Ⓑ Ⓒ Ⓓ
18 Ⓐ Ⓑ Ⓒ Ⓓ	48 Ⓐ Ⓑ Ⓒ Ⓓ	78 Ⓐ Ⓑ Ⓒ Ⓓ	108 Ⓐ Ⓑ Ⓒ Ⓓ
19 Ⓐ Ⓑ Ⓒ Ⓓ	49 Ⓐ Ⓑ Ⓒ Ⓓ	79 Ⓐ Ⓑ Ⓒ Ⓓ	109 Ⓐ Ⓑ Ⓒ Ⓓ
20 Ⓐ Ⓑ Ⓒ Ⓓ	50 Ⓐ Ⓑ Ⓒ Ⓓ	80 Ⓐ Ⓑ Ⓒ Ⓓ	110 Ⓐ Ⓑ Ⓒ Ⓓ
21 Ⓐ Ⓑ Ⓒ Ⓓ	51 Ⓐ Ⓑ Ⓒ Ⓓ	81 Ⓐ Ⓑ Ⓒ Ⓓ	111 Ⓐ Ⓑ Ⓒ Ⓓ
22 Ⓐ Ⓑ Ⓒ Ⓓ	52 Ⓐ Ⓑ Ⓒ Ⓓ	82 Ⓐ Ⓑ Ⓒ Ⓓ	112 Ⓐ Ⓑ Ⓒ Ⓓ
23 Ⓐ Ⓑ Ⓒ Ⓓ	53 Ⓐ Ⓑ Ⓒ Ⓓ	83 Ⓐ Ⓑ Ⓒ Ⓓ	113 Ⓐ Ⓑ Ⓒ Ⓓ
24 Ⓐ Ⓑ Ⓒ Ⓓ	54 Ⓐ Ⓑ Ⓒ Ⓓ	84 Ⓐ Ⓑ Ⓒ Ⓓ	114 Ⓐ Ⓑ Ⓒ Ⓓ
25 Ⓐ Ⓑ Ⓒ Ⓓ	55 Ⓐ Ⓑ Ⓒ Ⓓ	85 Ⓐ Ⓑ Ⓒ Ⓓ	115 Ⓐ Ⓑ Ⓒ Ⓓ
26 Ⓐ Ⓑ Ⓒ Ⓓ	56 Ⓐ Ⓑ Ⓒ Ⓓ	86 Ⓐ Ⓑ Ⓒ Ⓓ	116 Ⓐ Ⓑ Ⓒ Ⓓ
27 Ⓐ Ⓑ Ⓒ Ⓓ	57 Ⓐ Ⓑ Ⓒ Ⓓ	87 Ⓐ Ⓑ Ⓒ Ⓓ	117 Ⓐ Ⓑ Ⓒ Ⓓ
28 Ⓐ Ⓑ Ⓒ Ⓓ	58 Ⓐ Ⓑ Ⓒ Ⓓ	88 Ⓐ Ⓑ Ⓒ Ⓓ	118 Ⓐ Ⓑ Ⓒ Ⓓ
29 Ⓐ Ⓑ Ⓒ Ⓓ	59 Ⓐ Ⓑ Ⓒ Ⓓ	89 Ⓐ Ⓑ Ⓒ Ⓓ	119 Ⓐ Ⓑ Ⓒ Ⓓ
30 Ⓐ Ⓑ Ⓒ Ⓓ	60 Ⓐ Ⓑ Ⓒ Ⓓ	90 Ⓐ Ⓑ Ⓒ Ⓓ	120 Ⓐ Ⓑ Ⓒ Ⓓ

FOR ETS USE ONLY	R1	R2	R3	R4	R5	R6	TR	TCR	RS	CS

PRAXIS SPANISH: CONTENT KNOWLEDGE

90 Multiple-Choice Questions
Time—90 minutes

Recorded Portion of the Test

Section I	Interpretive Listening	Parts A, B, C
Section II	Structure of the Language (Grammatical Accuracy)	Part A

[The following directions will be heard on CD.]

This is the recorded portion of the study guide for the Praxis *Spanish: Content Knowledge* test. All the directions you will hear for this portion of the test are also printed in your test book.

In a moment, you will hear an introductory statement by two of the people who recorded this test. The purpose of this introduction is to familiarize you with the speakers' voices. Listen to the following passage.

Los alumnos tienen clases de lunes a viernes, excepto los días feriados. Este año, todos los alumnos saldrán temprano de la escuela el 20 y 27 de enero debido a que habrá conferencias para los profesores del colegio.

[Heard Twice]

GO ON TO THE NEXT PAGE

SECTION I

INTERPRETIVE LISTENING

Approximate time—23 minutes

Section I is designed to measure how well you understand spoken Spanish.

Part A: Questions 1–8

Directions: In Part A, you will hear short conversations between two people. After each conversation, you will hear one or more questions. The conversations and questions are not printed in the test book.

During the pause after each question, read the four answer choices printed in your test book and choose the <u>one</u> most appropriate answer. Indicate your choice on your answer sheet.

For example, you will hear:

[Recorded conversation and question]

In your test book you will read:

SAMPLE ANSWER

Ⓐ ● Ⓒ Ⓓ

    (A) Con la oficina de turismo.
    (B) Con la operadora de teléfono.
    (C) Con un agente de viajes.
    (D) Con el ayuntamiento de Bogotá.

Of the four answer choices, (B) is the most appropriate answer. Therefore, you would fill in space (B) on your answer sheet.

You may take notes, but <u>only</u> in your test book.

Now we will begin Part A with the conversation for Question Number 1.

1. (A) De una nueva publicación.
    (B) De una traducción.
    (C) De una representación teatral.
    (D) De un trabajo de investigación.

    _____

2. (A) Que quiere oírla tocar el piano.
    (B) Que ya no toca el piano.
    (C) Que ya no puede contar con sus amigos.
    (D) Que el piano de sus amigos no toca bien.

Las preguntas 3 y 4 se refieren a una conversación en un lugar público.

3. (A) En la oficina de un cirujano.
    (B) En la sala de un abogado.
    (C) En el consultorio de un óptico.
    (D) En la clínica de un dentista.

4. (A) Que le examinen.
    (B) Que le expliquen la cuenta.
    (C) Que le reparen algo.
    (D) Que le devuelvan dinero.

Las preguntas 5 y 6 se refieren a una conversación en una escuela.

5. (A) Matricular a su hija.
    (B) Saber el horario de la escuela.
    (C) Asistir a unas clases.
    (D) Tomar unas vacaciones.

6. (A) Unos cuadernos y fotocopias.
    (B) La partida de nacimiento.
    (C) Un certificado de salud y las notas.
    (D) El pago de la matrícula.

    _____

7. (A) Se lesionó.
    (B) Ganó un partido de tenis.
    (C) Salió en una fotografía.
    (D) Llegó tarde a un torneo.

    _____

8. (A) Ir a un parque.
    (B) Estacionar su auto.
    (C) Ver una exhibición de arte.
    (D) Escuchar música.

GO ON TO THE NEXT PAGE

Part B: Questions 9–15

Directions: In Part B, you will hear short narrations. The narrations are not printed in your test book. After each narration, you will hear one or more questions, which are printed in your test book.

During the pause after each question, read the four answer choices printed in your test book and choose the <u>one</u> most appropriate answer. Indicate your choice on your answer sheet.

For example, you will hear:

[Recorded narration and question]

In your test book you will read:

¿De qué se habla en el anuncio?

SAMPLE ANSWER

    (A) De un hotel.
    (B) De un concurso.
    (C) De una tienda.
    (D) De un viaje.

Of the four answer choices, (A) is the most appropriate answer. Therefore, you would fill in space (A) on your answer sheet.

You may take notes, but <u>only</u> in your test book.

Now we will begin Part B with the narration for Question Number 9.

La pregunta 9 se refiere a un anuncio en un autobús.

9. ¿Cuál es el propósito principal de este anuncio?

(A) Recordar a los turistas cuál va a ser el punto de reunión para volver al hotel.
(B) Explicar las actividades que realizarán los turistas.
(C) Dar información a los turistas acerca de los horarios de los autobuses.
(D) Informar a los turistas que no pueden visitar el museo por la mañana.

Las preguntas 10–12 se refieren a un comentario en la radio.

10. ¿A qué se dedicará este programa?

(A) A la salud.
(B) A la depresión.
(C) Al ejercicio.
(D) A las dietas.

11. ¿Cada cuánto tendrá lugar este programa?

(A) Todos los días.
(B) Una vez por semana.
(C) Cinco veces por semana.
(D) Cada seis meses.

12. ¿Cómo se puede obtener información adicional según este anuncio?

(A) Leyendo los folletos que han publicado.
(B) Escribiendo a la Universidad de San Juan.
(C) Consultando con los que han participado en el programa.
(D) Llamando a las oficinas del Centro Villanueva.

La pregunta 13 se refiere a las noticias financieras siguientes.

13. ¿Qué se sabe sobre las dos empresas?

(A) Que se han arruinado.
(B) Que se van a unir.
(C) Que la prensa local no les ha dado mucha publicidad.
(D) Que no tenían suficientes representantes en las reuniones.

Las preguntas 14–15 se refieren a un aviso en la radio.

14. ¿A quién está dirigido el aviso?

(A) A los empleados del gobierno.
(B) A los jóvenes que cambian de trabajo a menudo.
(C) A los propietarios de pequeñas empresas.
(D) A los trabajadores en busca de empleo.

15. ¿Qué hay que hacer para recibir ayuda?

(A) Hacer una llamada telefónica.
(B) Presentarse en la oficina.
(C) Escribir una carta.
(D) Contratar un abogado.

GO ON TO THE NEXT PAGE

Part C: Questions 16–24

Directions: In Part C, you will hear narrations and conversations that are longer than those in Parts A and B. The narrations and conversations are not printed in your test book. After each narration or conversation, you will hear several questions, which are printed in your test book.

During the pause after each question, read the four answer choices printed in your test book and choose the one most appropriate answer. Indicate your choice on your answer sheet.

There is no sample question for this part.

You may take notes, but only in your test book.

Now we will begin Part C with the narration for Questions 16–18.

Las preguntas 16–18 se refieren a un comentario en la televisión sobre la salud.

16. ¿Qué sugiere este comentario?

   (A) Recetar pocos medicamentos para tratar las enfermedades infantiles.
   (B) Estar al tanto de los últimos adelantos pediátricos.
   (C) Distinguir entre el tratamiento médico de un adulto y un niño.
   (D) Tener presente los servicios de emergencia para niños en la comunidad.

17. ¿Cómo deben tratarse los malestares de los niños?

   (A) Con terapia inmediata.
   (B) Tomando en serio cada síntoma.
   (C) Como síntomas pasajeros.
   (D) Sin muchos medicamentos.

18. ¿A quién se dirige este comentario?

   (A) A los maestros.
   (B) A los médicos.
   (C) A los padres.
   (D) A los enfermos.

Las preguntas 19–21 se refieren a unas mujeres que figuran en la historia cultural de América Latina.

19. ¿De qué nación provienen Sor Leonor de Ovando y Salomé Ureña?

   (A) Del Perú.
   (B) De México.
   (C) De El Salvador.
   (D) De la República Dominicana.

20. ¿Qué característica tenían en común Leonor de Ovando y Juana Inés de la Cruz?

   (A) Eran monjas.
   (B) Eran colegas.
   (C) Trataban los mismos temas.
   (D) Escribieron en el mismo año.

21. ¿Qué importancia tuvo Salomé Ureña en su país?

   (A) Fue la primera mujer que enseñó historia en Santo Domingo.
   (B) Mejoró las oportunidades de los trabajadores.
   (C) Mejoró el sistema de enseñanza de su país.
   (D) Fue la primera mujer que trabajó en el gobierno.

Las preguntas 22–24 se refieren a una conversación entre una madre y la maestra de matemáticas de su hijo.

22. Según la madre, ¿qué tipo de muchacho es Carlos?

    (A) Atlético.
    (B) Artístico.
    (C) Estudioso.
    (D) Despreocupado.

23. ¿Qué quiere discutir la madre con la maestra?

    (A) Las notas de Carlos.
    (B) Un programa de verano para Carlos.
    (C) La tarea de Carlos.
    (D) La mejor universidad para Carlos.

24. ¿Qué le aconseja la maestra a la Sra. Suárez?

    (A) Que Carlos repita un curso de matemáticas.
    (B) Que Carlos participe en más actividades.
    (C) Que apoye los deseos de Carlos.
    (D) Que envíe una solicitud pronto.

GO ON TO THE NEXT PAGE

SECTION II

STRUCTURE OF THE LANGUAGE (Grammatical Accuracy)

Approximate time—26 minutes

Part A (recorded portion)—3 minutes

Parts B, C, and D—23 minutes

Section II is designed to measure your knowledge of the structure of the Spanish language.

Part A: Questions 25–31

Directions: In Part A, you will hear selections spoken by students who are learning Spanish and who make errors in their speech. The selections are not printed in your test book. After hearing a selection, you will hear one or more excerpts from the selection. Each excerpt contains only <u>one</u> error. You will be asked to identify, correct, or describe the type of error in the excerpt. When answering each question, consider the error in the context of the entire selection. The questions are printed in your test book.

During the pause after each question, read the four answer choices printed in your test book and choose the <u>one</u> most appropriate answer. Indicate your choice on your answer sheet.

For example, you will hear:

[Recorded selection and question]

Then you will hear again:

[Recorded excerpt]

In your test book you will read:

Identify the error in the following excerpt.

(A) *Hace*
(B) *tiempo*
(C) *te*
(D) *vi*

SAMPLE ANSWER

Ⓐ Ⓑ Ⓒ ⬤

Of the four answer choices, (D) is the most appropriate answer. Therefore, you would fill in space (D) on your answer sheet.

You may take notes, but <u>only</u> in your test book.

Now we will begin Part A with the selection for Questions 25–27.

Questions 25–27 refer to the following conversation between two friends who decide to take a shortcut through the woods to visit a friend and who then get lost.

25. Correct the error in the following excerpt by choosing the appropriate revision.

    (A) Revise *oyes* to *oye*
    (B) Revise *algo* to *nada.*
    (C) Revise *o* to *ni.*
    (D) Revise *algún* to *alguna.*

26. Correct the error in the following excerpt by choosing the appropriate revision.

    (A) Revise *Todavía* to *Porque.*
    (B) Revise *se ve* to *ve.*
    (C) Revise *oyen* to *oye.*
    (D) Revise *nada* to *ninguna.*

27. Correct the error in the following excerpt by choosing the appropriate revision.

    (A) Revise *Pero* to *Tampoco.*
    (B) Revise *debamos* to *deberíamos.*
    (C) Revise *llegado* to *llegados.*
    (D) Revise *a* to *en.*

Questions 28–31 are based on the following conversation between a nurse and a patient in a doctor's office.

28. Identify the error in the following excerpt.

    (A) *Buenos*
    (B) *días*
    (C) *En qué*
    (D) *ayudarlo*

29. Identify the error in the following excerpt.

    (A) *Tuve*
    (B) *cita*
    (C) *doctora*
    (D) *Méndez Rivera*

30. Identify the error in the following excerpt.

    (A) *Usted es*
    (B) *la señora*
    (C) *está citada*
    (D) *medio*

31. Identify the error in the following excerpt.

    (A) *llegado*
    (B) *un poco*
    (C) *temprano*
    (D) *Siéntate*

STOP.

THIS IS THE END OF THE RECORDED PORTION OF THE TEST.

AT THE ACTUAL TEST ADMINISTRATION, YOU MUST NOT TURN THE PAGE UNTIL YOU ARE TOLD TO DO SO.

END OF RECORDING.

Part B: Questions 32–39

Directions: In Part B, you will read paragraphs written by students who are learning Spanish. Each paragraph contains errors. You will be asked to identify, correct, or describe the type of error in some of the sentences from each paragraph; each of these sentences contains only <u>one</u> error. When answering each question, consider the error in the context of the entire paragraph.

For each question, choose the <u>one</u> most appropriate answer from the four answer choices printed in your test book. Indicate your choice on your answer sheet.

For example:

¡Apúrate, Juan! Deje el trabajo para más tarde.

Identify the error in the sentence.

SAMPLE ANSWER

● Ⓑ Ⓒ Ⓓ

(A) *Deje*
(B) *el trabajo*
(C) *para*
(D) *más tarde*

Of the four answer choices, (A) is the most appropriate answer. Therefore, you would fill in space (A) on your answer sheet.

You may take notes, but <u>only</u> in your test book.

Questions 32–35 refer to the following passage about two people who have lost their keys.

(1) Todas las ventanas de atrás estaba también cerradas. (2) "¿Adónde pusiste la llave?" le pregunté a Manolito. (3) Inesperadamente comenzó a llorar. (4) Los hoteles más cercanos quedando a treinta kilómetros. (5) Manolito sabía que sin duda nos teníamos quedar afuera toda la noche.

32. Identify the error in sentence 1.

    (A) *Todas*
    (B) *atrás*
    (C) *estaba*
    (D) *cerradas*

33. Identify the error in sentence 2.

    (A) *Adónde*
    (B) *pusiste*
    (C) *le*
    (D) *pregunté*

34. In sentence 4, the word *quedando* is used incorrectly. Which of the following is correct in the context of the passage?

    (A) *quedo*
    (B) *queden*
    (C) *quedaban*
    (D) *quedaría*

35. Identify the error in sentence 5.

    (A) *sabía*
    (B) *sin duda*
    (C) *teníamos quedar*
    (D) *afuera*

Questions 36–39 refer to the following passage about a trip.

(1) Salimos en el tren de las seis, dejando tras la ciudad y atravesando la sabana hacia el norte, siempre con la puesta del sol al lado izquierdo. (2) En el ambiente del vagón estaba expectativa, como un nerviosismo controlado. (3) Los pasajeros parecían descansando después de la confusión del andén. (4) Cuando llegamos al río, anunciaron que la puente estaba dañado y que teníamos que regresar a Bogotá.

36. Identify the error in sentence 1.

    (A) *dejando*
    (B) *tras*
    (C) *hacia*
    (D) *la puesta*

37. Identify the error in sentence 2.

    (A) *ambiente*
    (B) *estaba*
    (C) *como*
    (D) *controlado*

38. In sentence 3, the word *descansando* is used incorrectly. Which of the following is correct in the context of the passage?

    (A) *descansen*
    (B) *descansaban*
    (C) *descansado*
    (D) *descansar*

39. Identify the error in sentence 4.

    (A) *anunciaron*
    (B) *la puente*
    (C) *que teníamos que*
    (D) *a Bogotá*

Part C: Questions 40–44

Directions: In Part C, you will read questions about the structure of the Spanish language. For each question, choose the <u>one</u> most appropriate answer from the four answer choices printed in your test book. Indicate your choice on your answer sheet.

For example:

Which of the following is a noun suffix that indicates a place where business or work is performed?

SAMPLE ANSWER

(A) *-ero*
(B) *-istas*
(C) *-ismo*
(D) *-ería*

Of the four answer choices, (D) is the most appropriate answer. Therefore, you would fill in space (D) on your answer sheet.

You may take notes, but <u>only</u> in your test book.

40. Which of the following Spanish words has the same meaning as the underlined words in the sentence "They plan to attend a play tonight"?

    (A) *Atender*
    (B) *Asistir*
    (C) *Tender*
    (D) *Presentar*

41. Which of the following changes should be made to the name *Fernández* when the family name is used to refer to more than one person?

    (A) Add the definite article *los*.
    (B) Add the preposition *con*.
    (C) Add the preposition *de*.
    (D) Add the plural suffix *-es*.

42. Which of the following adjectives would need to be changed to modify a feminine noun?

    (A) *Dulce*
    (B) *Hipócrita*
    (C) *Feroz*
    (D) *Alemán*

43. The absolute superlative, or greatest degree, of an adjective is indicated by

    (A) *-ible*
    (B) *-ísimo*
    (C) *-ona*
    (D) *-able*

44. Which of the following questions does NOT ask about how a person feels?

    (A) *¿Cómo te sientes?*
    (B) *¿Cómo eres?*
    (C) *¿Cómo te encuentras?*
    (D) *¿Cómo estás?*

Part D: Questions 45–50

Directions: In Part D, you will read sentences or paragraphs from which words or phrases have been omitted. Each sentence is followed by four possibilities for completing the sentence. For each blank, choose the <u>one</u> answer that results in the best sentence or paragraph in written Spanish. When choosing your answer, consider it in the context of the entire sentence or paragraph. Indicate your choice on your answer sheet.

For example:

¡Qué suerte tuvimos! Compramos el carro nuevo
por menos _____ pensábamos.

(A) de que
(B) de lo que
(C) de
(D) que

SAMPLE ANSWER

Ⓐ ● Ⓒ Ⓓ

Of the four answer choices, (B) is the most appropriate answer. Therefore, you would fill in space (B) on your answer sheet.

You may take notes, but <u>only</u> in your test book.

El profesor apreció mucho (45) bien escrita que estaba la novela que (46) de leer. Empezó entonces a pensar en las otras obras que (47) de esta autora para recomendárselas a sus alumnos.

45. (A) tan
    (B) que tan
    (C) lo
    (D) que lo

46. (A) acaba
    (B) acabó
    (C) acababa
    (D) acabe

47. (A) leían
    (B) lea
    (C) han leído
    (D) había leído

Nuestro viaje resultó ser un fracaso completo, a (48) los planes minuciosos que (49) . Todo esto fue debido a contratiempos inesperados, imposibles (50) anticipar.

48. (A) fin de que
    (B) menos que
    (C) pesar de
    (D) manera de

49. (A) hacíamos
    (B) hagamos
    (C) habríamos hecho
    (D) habíamos hecho

50. (A) de
    (B) a
    (C) al
    (D) en

SECTION III

INTERPRETIVE READING

Suggested Time—26 minutes

Section III is designed to measure how well you can understand written Spanish.

Section III: Questions 51–74

Directions: In Section III, you will read several selections or passages in Spanish. Each selection or passage is followed by questions. For each question, choose the <u>one</u> most appropriate answer from the four answer choices printed in your test book. Indicate your choice on your answer sheet.

When answering the questions, consider them in the context of the entire selection or passage. Base each answer <u>only</u> on what is stated or implied in the selection or passage. There is no sample question for this part.

You may take notes, but <u>only</u> in your test book.

Las preguntas 51–56 se refieren al siguiente pasaje literario.

Cada vez que crujía una ramita, o croaba una rana, o vibraban los vidrios de la cocina que
Línea estaba al fondo de la huerta, el viejecito saltaba con agilidad de su asiento improvisado, que era
(5) una piedra chata, y espiaba ansiosamente entre el follaje. Pero el niño aún no aparecía. A través de las ventanas del comedor, abiertas a la pérgola, veía en cambio las luces de la araña encendida hacía rato, y bajo ella sombras
(10) imprecisas que se deslizaban de un lado a otro, con las cortinas, lentamente. Había sido corto de vista desde joven, de modo que eran inútiles sus esfuerzos por comprobar si ya cenaban o si aquellas sombras inquietas provenían de los
(15) árboles más altos. Regresó a su asiento y esperó. Los insectos pululaban, y los manoteos desesperados de don Eulogio en torno del rostro, no conseguían evitarlos. El entusiasmo y la excitación que mantuvieron su cuerpo
(20) dispuesto y febril durante el día habían decaído y sentía ahora cansancio y algo de tristeza. Le molestaba la oscuridad del vasto jardín y lo atormentaba la imagen, persistente, humillante, de alguien que de pronto lo sorprendiera en su
(25) escondrijo. "¿Qué hace usted en la huerta a estas horas, don Eulogio?" Y vendrían su hijo y su hija política, convencidos de que estaba loco. Sacudido por un temblor nervioso, volvió la cabeza y adivinó entre los macizos de
(30) crisantemos, de nardos y de rosales, el diminuto sendero que llegaba a la puerta falsa esquivando el palomar. Se tranquilizó apenas, al recordar haber comprobado tres veces que la puerta estaba abierta, con el pestillo corrido, y
(35) que en unos segundos podía escurrirse hacia la calle sin ser visto.

51. ¿Dónde tiene lugar la acción en este pasaje?

(A) En un parque
(B) En un jardín
(C) En una playa
(D) En un restaurante

52. ¿Cuándo saltaba el viejecito de su asiento?

(A) Cuando veía aparecer al niño
(B) Cuando aparecía la araña
(C) Cuando oía algún ruido
(D) Cuando encendían las luces

53. ¿Qué parecía hacer el viejecito?

(A) Mover las cortinas
(B) Hablar con su hija política
(C) Abrir las ventanas
(D) Esperar a alguien

54. El viejecito no podía explicar de dónde provenían las sombras porque

(A) estaba muy lejos de la casa
(B) no veía bien
(C) había demasiados árboles
(D) llovía mucho

55. ¿Por qué hacía gestos con sus manos don Eulogio?

(A) Porque los insectos le molestaban
(B) Porque las cortinas le estorbaban la vista
(C) Porque había muchas telarañas
(D) Porque quería atraer la atención de su hijo

56. ¿En qué estado de ánimo estaba don Eulogio?

(A) Bastante nervioso
(B) Indiferente a su situación
(C) Igual que siempre
(D) Muy entusiasmado

Las preguntas 57–62 se refieren al siguiente fragmento de una entrevista con Octavio Paz.

"Como muchísima gente en el siglo XX, yo he sufrido y gozado la suerte de los emigrantes. Cuando yo era niño mi padre tuvo que dejar
Línea México. Era la época de la revolución mexicana
(5)   y mi padre, que había participado en política y colaborado con el grupo de la Convención y con Emiliano Zapata, tuvo que salir huyendo. Fue a los Estados Unidos como representante personal del general Zapata. Nosotros tuvimos
(10)   que unirnos a él un año después. Yo era muy niño entonces. Atravesamos todo el país en tren. Todavía los trenes iban muy escoltados por soldados porque había frecuentemente tiroteos con las guerrillas. Para mí, éste fue un
(15)   recuerdo inolvidable, un viaje terrible de más de una semana desde la Ciudad de México hasta la frontera, donde nos estaba esperando mi padre. De ahí fuimos a Los Ángeles, donde vivimos dos años. Desde niño tuve que vivir la
(20)   suerte del refugiado, tuve que aprender a hablar otro idioma y a saber enfrentarme a otros niños distintos a mí.
"Los que escribimos en español tenemos la ventaja de que tenemos cerca de medio mundo
(25)   para emigrar. Pero, aún cuando se trata de la amenaza de la pérdida del idioma . . . en algunos casos ha traído hasta ganancias; por ejemplo, el caso de Nabokov o de Joseph Conrad, que cambiaron de idioma. Juan Ramón
(30)   Jiménez se quejaba de que los nombres de los árboles en Estados Unidos eran distintos a los nombres en España, pero a mí me parece, sin embargo, que es maravilloso que los mismos objetos tengan nombres distintos. Me parece un
(35)   tema hasta poético. Yo no estoy en contra. Los escritores a veces hemos emigrado por voluntad propia. Yo he vivido la mitad de mi vida fuera de México, trabajando como profesor, como periodista, como diplomático. Dejé México en
(40)   1943 y no volví a instalarme hasta 1970, y, sin embargo, escribí mucho sobre México porque México se convirtió en una pasión, una pasión doble, una pasión llena de disputas y de polémicas, pero no hubiera sido posible sin
(45)   estas ausencias. Cervantes, nuestro gran modelo, viajó. Los españoles viajaron mucho; cuando dejaron de viajar escribieron menos bien".

57. ¿Por qué se fue de México el padre de Octavio Paz?

(A) Porque colaboraba con representantes de los Estados Unidos
(B) A causa de sus alianzas políticas
(C) Porque quería aprender otro idioma
(D) A causa de su deseo de reunirse con su familia

58. ¿Por qué fue inolvidable el primer viaje de Octavio Paz a los Estados Unidos?

(A) Por la velocidad en que viajaba el tren
(B) Por el hermoso panorama que observó
(C) Porque tuvo la compañía de su padre durante toda la semana
(D) Porque fue un viaje largo y peligroso

59. Según el pasaje, ¿qué beneficio le trajo a Octavio Paz su temprano exilio?

(A) Representó a su país en un congreso de autores.
(B) Aprendió a expresarse en una nueva lengua.
(C) Pudo pagarse una buena educación universitaria.
(D) Llegó a establecer contacto con escritores de otros países.

60. Según Octavio Paz, el hecho de que los mismos objetos tengan nombres distintos es

(A) un desafío común a todos los escritores
(B) un tema difícil de explicar
(C) un beneficio para los escritores
(D) una dificultad lingüística

61. Según el pasaje, ¿qué le pasó al autor después de emigrar de su país de origen?

    (A) Pensó intensamente en su tierra natal.
    (B) Recordó la tranquilidad y la paz de su niñez.
    (C) Careció de antecedentes literarios.
    (D) Dejó de pensar en la política.

62. Según Octavio Paz, los escritores escriben mejor cuando

    (A) escriben tanta prosa como poesía
    (B) tienen formación periodística
    (C) tienen oportunidad de viajar
    (D) están envueltos en muchas polémicas

Las preguntas 63–68 se refieren al siguiente pasaje literario.

    Cuando Víctor Erice entró, hace diecisiete años, en el jardín del colegio de Ana buscando una niña que pudiera interpretar un papel en *El*
Línea *espíritu de la colmena*, seguramente no sabía
(5) que, con ello, estaba moviendo los hilos de una vida, cambiando el destino y la suerte de una persona. Ella ni siquiera se acuerda de aquel encuentro. Era demasiado pequeña. Pero él no debió olvidar la cara de aquella personita a la
(10) que descubrió apartada, jugando sola, con esos ojos inocentes y expresivos que cautivaron a medio mundo.
    Cualquiera podría pensar que Ana Torrent estaba acostumbrada, desde su más tierna
(15) infancia, a moverse en el medio en que trabaja. "Pero la verdad es que no. Yo no interpretaba nada. Me decían: ponte aquí y di esto. Y yo repetía la frase como me salía y miraba hacia donde me decían. Así de fácil. Puede que sí me
(20) sirviera para acostumbrarme a la cámara, a perderle miedo, pero en cuanto a técnica . . . nada".
    Parece increíble pero Ana comenzó a trabajar en el cine mucho antes de tener
(25) conciencia de lo que hacía. Sus primeros recuerdos, más o menos hilvanados, están ligados al rodaje de aquella película en la que lo pasó tan bien. Su padre procuró por todos los medios que aquella aventura no le afectara y,
(30) cuando Carlos Saura se presentó en casa para convencerle de que la niña hiciera *Cría cuervos*, se negó. "Pensaba que, bueno, ya había trabajado en una película, y que eso era suficiente. Mi familia no tenía nada que ver con
(35) ese mundo, lo desconocían por completo y mi padre tenía miedo de que me convirtiera en la típica niña de cine que falta a clase, se hace muy famosa, pierde la relación con sus compañeros y sus hermanos y se diferencia de
(40) ellos porque se siente artista". De eso sí se acuerda Ana, que tenía ocho años y le daba exactamente igual hacer o no la película.

63. ¿Qué buscaba Víctor Erice hace diecisiete años?

    (A) Una actriz
    (B) Una profesora de colegio
    (C) Una jardinera
    (D) Una productora de cine

64. Ana no recuerda su primer encuentro con Víctor Erice porque

    (A) el encuentro fue muy breve
    (B) no le vio la cara
    (C) no habló mucho con él
    (D) ella era muy joven

65. ¿Qué aspecto de Ana Torrent le impresionó mucho a Erice?

    (A) Su voz
    (B) Su personalidad
    (C) Su rostro
    (D) Su memoria

66. ¿Cuál de las siguientes declaraciones describe mejor la preparación de Ana?

    (A) Tenía poco entrenamiento formal.
    (B) Había estudiado música por varios años.
    (C) Le habían dado clases de modelar.
    (D) Había aprendido mucho de sus padres.

67. El padre estaba preocupado por el tipo de trabajo que Ana hacía porque no quería

    (A) que el trabajo la perjudicara
    (B) estar separado de su hija
    (C) negarle a su hija lo que le gustaba
    (D) que recordara los malos momentos del rodaje

68. ¿Cuál fue la actitud de Ana cuando le pidieron que hiciera una segunda película?

    (A) Quería esperar hasta terminar sus estudios.
    (B) No le dio mucha importancia.
    (C) Demostró su admiración a Saura.
    (D) No quería que su madre actuara con ella.

Las preguntas 69–74 se refieren al siguiente pasaje.

Marina Mayoral se dio a conocer como novelista en castellano en 1979 con su novela *Cándida otra vez*, ganando el segundo premio de la
Línea Editorial Ámbito Literario. Al mismo tiempo que
(5) su narrativa parece tener una fuente común con el folclore de su nativa Galicia por su énfasis en el acto de contar y sus elementos de leyenda y misterio, representa una ruptura con varias tradiciones literarias: el cuento de hadas, el
(10) romance, la novela realista y la Generación del '98. Sus novelas y sus cuentos son testimonio de una prosa rica y sugestiva en la que mezcla varios ingredientes literarios. En parte es la mezcla misma la que apunta hacia una revisión de fórmulas
(15) narrativas tradicionales y por otra parte es la inversión de los elementos de estas fórmulas. Su material se centra en la época contemporánea de Galicia y Madrid, sugiriendo constantemente un contraste entre los dos recintos geográficos, entre lo
(20) tradicional y lo moderno. Lo familiar y lo ancestral son aspectos tradicionales que se convierten en anomalías y perversiones en el mundo de hoy.
Cada una de sus novelas es en realidad una serie de cuentos, versiones diferentes y dispares de los
(25) mismos incidentes, repetidos infinitamente sin llegar a ninguna versión definitiva. Mayoral pide prestado elementos de los géneros populares como la novela rosa y la novela policíaca para atraer al lector y también para crear una compleja narrativa
(30) de difícil clasificación. Es una lectura amena por los elementos populares que introduce, pero también mucho más profunda y satisfactoria que la lectura popular.
Mayoral cree que el cuento es un género
(35) literario injustamente despreciado. Su propia contribución a la cuentística española es notable. Como en sus novelas, tiene la maestría narrativa de poder incorporar complejos elementos en sus cuentos cortos donde demuestra una
(40) autoconsciencia del acto narrativo y también una tendencia a invertir papeles y situaciones tradicionales, rompiendo barreras literarias y sociales. Su hábil combinación de elementos genéricos y técnicas narrativas cruza una frontera
(45) para llegar a un lugar en el que hay plena libertad literaria que al mismo tiempo responde al primer requisito de toda narración—contar una historia que interese al lector. Simultáneamente proyecta

vidas modernas que se encuentran atrapadas en una
(50) tensión entre las normas tradicionales y restrictivas y la vida moderna; el camino de sus personajes queda sin solución definitiva.

69. ¿Cuál es el propósito principal de este pasaje?

(A) Estudiar los cuentos de Marina Mayoral
(B) Describir el contraste entre el enfoque literario en Galicia y en el resto de España
(C) Reseñar la producción literaria de Marina Mayoral
(D) Difundir un género literario poco apreciado

70. ¿Por qué se menciona en el pasaje la Generación del '98 ?

(A) Para hacer resaltar su compromiso con un movimiento literario del siglo XIX
(B) Para enfatizar cómo la autora se ha separado de convenciones literarias previas
(C) Para unir la técnica literaria de Mayoral con la de generaciones anteriores
(D) Para hacer una distinción entre la generación del '98 y otras tradiciones literarias populares

71. ¿Qué importancia le da Mayoral a los géneros populares?

(A) Los considera como géneros literarios de poco valor.
(B) Los incorpora en su obra para crear una narrativa original.
(C) Los considera de difícil clasificación.
(D) Los define como anomalías de las tradiciones literarias.

72. ¿Por qué se mencionan en el pasaje la novela rosa y la novela policíaca?

(A) Para ilustrar ciertos géneros literarios que inspiraron la obra de Mayoral
(B) Para contrastar sus diferentes estilos narrativos con los de Mayoral
(C) Porque son dos tipos de novela que Mayoral escribe
(D) Porque son más interesantes que las novelas de Mayoral

73. Mayoral opina que el cuento es un género

   (A) inapreciado
   (B) repetitivo
   (C) anticuado
   (D) complejo

74. Según el pasaje, ¿cuál debería ser el objetivo
    primordial de toda narración?

   (A) Crear una prosa original
   (B) Romper las barreras literarias
   (C) Alcanzar plena libertad de expresión
   (D) Cautivar la atención del lector

SECTION IV

CULTURAL PERSPECTIVES

Suggested Time—15 minutes

Section IV is designed to measure your knowledge of the cultures of Spanish-speaking countries and regions.

Section IV: Questions 75–90

Directions: For each question in Section IV, choose the <u>one</u> most appropriate answer from the four answer choices printed in your test book. Indicate your choice on your answer sheet.

For example:

Un magnífico ejemplo de la arquitectura
Inca es

(A) Chichén Itzá
(B) Machu Picchu
(C) Tikal
(D) Teotihuacán

SAMPLE ANSWER

Ⓐ ● Ⓒ Ⓓ

Of the four answer choices, (B) is the most appropriate answer. Therefore, you would fill in space (B) on your answer sheet.

You may take notes, but <u>only</u> in your test book.

75. El nombre de Emiliano Zapata está directamente asociado

    (A) a la revolución mexicana de 1910
    (B) al populismo argentino de los años 50
    (C) a la revolución cubana de 1959
    (D) al gobierno militar chileno de los años 70

76. ¿Cuáles de los siguientes pintores son de México?

    (A) Frida Kahlo y Diego Rivera
    (B) Pablo Picasso y Joan Miró
    (C) El Greco y Francisco de Goya
    (D) Salvador Dalí y Fernando Botero

77. ¿Cuál es la obra que dio origen a la novela picaresca en el siglo XVI?

    (A) *Don Quixote de la Mancha*
    (B) *Cien Años de Soledad*
    (C) *Don Segundo Sombra*
    (D) *Lazarillo de Tormes*

78. ¿Cuál de las siguientes civilizaciones se asocia con Perú?

    (A) Los olmecas
    (B) Los aztecas
    (C) Los incas
    (D) Los mayas

79. Todas las siguientes ciudades se asocian con los moros EXCEPTO

    (A) Córdoba
    (B) Granada
    (C) Sevilla
    (D) Barcelona

La pregunta 80 se refiere al siguiente artículo de un boletín interno de una compañía.

Rodeada del afecto de sus seres queridos, durante alegre fiesta, celebró sus quince años la ahijada de nuestro colega, el Ing. Sergio Gómez, la gentil señorita Zaida Núñez, hija de Ana Blanco de Núñez.

80. El artículo se refiere a

    (A) un ascenso
    (B) un retiro
    (C) un cumpleaños
    (D) un aniversario de bodas

81. ¿Cuál de los siguientes personajes se asocia con el movimiento de independencia de la Argentina del siglo XIX?

    (A) Porfirio Díaz
    (B) Simón Bolívar
    (C) Fulgencio Batista
    (D) José de San Martin

82. Las porciones pequeñas de comida ligera que se sirven en los bares y los cafés de España son

    (A) las onces
    (B) las tapas
    (C) la comida
    (D) las meriendas

83. Un crucero por el Mar Caribe haría escala en los siguientes puertos EXCEPTO

    (A) San Juan, Puerto Rico
    (B) Santo Domingo
    (C) Cozumel
    (D) Palma de Mallorca

Las preguntas 84–85 se refieren al siguiente mapa de Sudamérica en el cual se han enumerado nueve países.

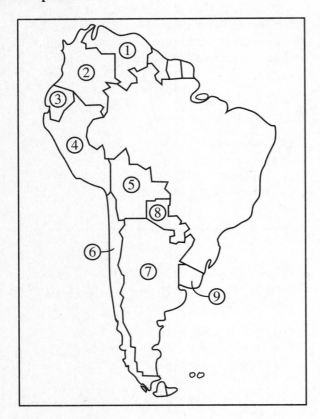

84. ¿Entre cuáles de los siguientes países corre el Río de la Plata?

    (A) 2 y 4
    (B) 4 y 5
    (C) 6 y 7
    (D) 7 y 9

85. ¿En cuál de los siguientes países está Machu Picchu?

    (A) 3
    (B) 4
    (C) 5
    (D) 6

86. ¿Con cuál de los siguientes países se asocia a José Martí?

   (A) Nicaragua
   (B) Costa Rica
   (C) Cuba
   (D) La República Dominicana

87. ¿En cuál de los siguientes países se encuentran Campeche, Chiapas, Guanajuato y Oaxaca?

   (A) México
   (B) Honduras
   (C) Costa Rica
   (D) Guatemala

88. Gabriela Mistral, Pablo Neruda y Gabriel García Márquez, entre otros, han logrado fama mundial por ser

   (A) recipientes del Premio Nobel
   (B) presidentes de su país natal
   (C) cantantes de música popular
   (D) deportistas de primera categoría

89. El palacio de la Alhambra y la mezquita de Córdoba son algunos de los ejemplos del impacto que tuvo en España la cultura

   (A) griega
   (B) romana
   (C) árabe
   (D) judía

90. ¿Cuál de los siguientes bailes tiene su origen en la Argentina?

   (A) El bolero
   (B) La samba
   (C) El tango
   (D) El merengue

Chapter 6
Right Answers and Explanations for the Practice Questions—*Spanish: Content Knowledge*

▶   ▶   ▶   ▶   ▶   ▶   ▶   ▶   ▶   ▶   ▶   ▶

Now that you have answered all of the practice questions, you can check your work. Compare your answers to the multiple-choice questions with the correct answers in the table below.

Question Number	Correct Answer	Content Category
1	C	Interpretive Listening—Short Conversation
2	B	Interpretive Listening—Short Conversation
3	C	Interpretive Listening—Short Conversation
4	C	Interpretive Listening—Short Conversation
5	A	Interpretive Listening—Short Conversation
6	C	Interpretive Listening—Short Conversation
7	A	Interpretive Listening—Short Conversation
8	D	Interpretive Listening—Short Conversation
9	B	Interpretive Listening—Short Narration
10	A	Interpretive Listening—Short Narration
11	B	Interpretive Listening—Short Narration
12	D	Interpretive Listening—Short Narration
13	B	Interpretive Listening—Short Narration
14	C	Interpretive Listening—Short Narration
15	B	Interpretive Listening—Short Narration
16	C	Interpretive Listening—Long Narration
17	B	Interpretive Listening—Long Narration
18	C	Interpretive Listening—Long Narration
19	D	Interpretive Listening—Long Narration
20	A	Interpretive Listening—Long Narration
21	C	Interpretive Listening—Long Narration
22	C	Interpretive Listening—Long Conversation
23	B	Interpretive Listening—Long Conversation
24	C	Interpretive Listening—Long Conversation
25	D	Structure of the Language—Speech
26	C	Structure of the Language—Speech
27	B	Structure of the Language—Speech
28	D	Structure of the Language—Speech
29	A	Structure of the Language—Speech
30	D	Structure of the Language—Speech
31	D	Structure of the Language—Speech
32	C	Structure of the Language—Writing
33	A	Structure of the Language—Writing
34	C	Structure of the Language—Writing
35	C	Structure of the Language—Writing
36	B	Structure of the Language—Writing
37	B	Structure of the Language—Writing
38	D	Structure of the Language—Writing

Question Number	Correct Answer	Content Category
39	B	Structure of the Language—Writing
40	B	Structure of the Language—Language Analysis
41	A	Structure of the Language—Language Analysis
42	D	Structure of the Language—Language Analysis
43	B	Structure of the Language—Language Analysis
44	B	Structure of the Language—Language Analysis
45	C	Structure of the Language—Grammar
46	C	Structure of the Language—Grammar
47	D	Structure of the Language—Grammar
48	C	Structure of the Language—Grammar
49	D	Structure of the Language—Grammar
50	A	Structure of the Language—Grammar
51	B	Interpretive Reading—Content and Organization
52	C	Interpretive Reading—Content and Organization
53	D	Interpretive Reading—Content and Organization
54	B	Interpretive Reading—Implied Content
55	A	Interpretive Reading—Implied Content
56	A	Interpretive Reading—Content and Organization
57	B	Interpretive Reading—Content and Organization
58	D	Interpretive Reading—Content and Organization
59	B	Interpretive Reading—Content and Organization
60	C	Interpretive Reading—Content and Organization
61	A	Interpretive Reading—Content and Organization
62	C	Interpretive Reading—Implied Content
63	A	Interpretive Reading—Content and Organization

Question Number	Correct Answer	Content Category
64	D	Interpretive Reading—Content and Organization
65	C	Interpretive Reading—Content and Organization
66	A	Interpretive Reading—Implied Content
67	A	Interpretive Reading—Implied Content
68	B	Interpretive Reading—Content and Organization
69	C	Interpretive Reading—Content and Organization
70	B	Interpretive Reading—Content and Organization
71	B	Interpretive Reading—Content and Organization
72	A	Interpretive Reading—Implied Content
73	A	Interpretive Reading—Content and Organization
74	D	Interpretive Reading—Implied Content
75	A	Cultural Perspectives—History
76	A	Cultural Perspectives—Literature and the Arts
77	D	Cultural Perspectives—Literature and the Arts

Question Number	Correct Answer	Content Category
78	C	Cultural Perspectives—History
79	D	Cultural Perspectives—Geography
80	C	Cultural Perspectives—Lifestyles and Societies
81	D	Cultural Perspectives—History
82	B	Cultural Perspectives—Lifestyles and Societies
83	D	Cultural Perspectives—Geography
84	D	Cultural Perspectives—Geography
85	B	Cultural Perspectives—Geography
86	C	Cultural Perspectives—Literature and the Arts
87	A	Cultural Perspectives—Geography
88	A	Cultural Perspectives—Literature and the Arts
89	C	Cultural Perspectives—History
90	C	Cultural Perspectives—Lifestyles and Societies

Explanations of Right Answers

1. This question tests your listening comprehension of spoken Spanish. The correct choice is (C) because you hear the following references: *la mejor interpretación, ha hecho el papel*, and *obra*. (A) and (B) are related to written material, and, although you hear *Don Quijote* mentioned, the cues refer to a play rather than a novel. There is no evidence to support choice (D). The correct answer, therefore, is (C).

2. This question tests your listening skills and specifically focuses on your ability to distinguish different conjugated forms. In the conversation, the woman uses the verb *tocar* in the present form (*tocas*), asking the man if he plays the piano. He replies using the verb *tocar* in the imperfect form (*tocaba*), indicating the action is past, that he used to play. The correct answer, therefore, is (B).

3. This question tests your understanding of standard spoken Spanish. In the conversation the man explains that a lens in his glasses fell out and needs to be repaired. Of the choices offered, the only logical place where the repairs can be done is choice (C). Therefore, the correct answer is (C).

4. This question tests listening comprehension of high-frequency vocabulary; the correct answer is stated explicitly when the man asks the woman to fix the glasses. *Arreglar* is a synonym of *reparar*. There is no reference to an examination, or to the cost of the repairs, so (A), (B), and (D) are not plausible. The correct answer, therefore, is (C).

5. This question tests your listening skills and knowledge of Spanish vocabulary. Reference is made in the conversation to *documentación . . . para que mi hija ingrese en esta escuela*. These are words associated with *matrícula*, choice (A). Choices (B) and (D) refer to school scheduling and taking vacations, and choice (C) refers to the man's taking classes, not to his daughter. Therefore, the correct answer is (A).

6. This question also tests listening skills and specific Spanish vocabulary. In the conversation, two documents are required: *las calificaciones* and *el registro de vacunas*. Another way of saying this is *un certificado de salud y las notas*, as in choice (C). The other choices refer to notebooks and photocopies, a birth certificate, and payment of tuition. Therefore, the correct answer is (C).

7. This question tests your ability to distinguish fine-point details in spoken Spanish. In choice (A), the word *lesionó* refers to an injury, and in the conversation the woman asks *¿Cómo se lastimó usted?* The man explains that he fell (*Me caí . . .*) while he was playing tennis. Choice (B) does mention tennis, but there is a reference only to the outcome of the game. Choice (C) uses the word *fotografía* as a distractor since it sounds like *radiografía* (X-ray); a listener might get confused between the words, which have similar endings. There is no evidence that the game was part of a tournament, which discounts choice (D). The correct answer, therefore, is (A).

8. This question tests your skill in listening for specific information. At the beginning of the dialogue, the woman makes reference to going to a concert, and therefore to choice (D), *escuchar música*, which is the correct answer. There is no reference to choice (A). Choice (B) is a tempting choice, because the man in the dialogue speaks about traffic being heavy and possible difficulty in finding a parking spot. Choice (C) is also a tempting choice, because, according to the woman, the concert will take place in the *Palacio de Bellas Artes*.

9. This question tests your skill in listening for main ideas. Choice (A) can be eliminated because a specific meeting point is never mentioned. Choices (C) and (D) can be eliminated because there is no mention of a specific bus schedule or of museum visiting hours. Choice (B) reflects the main purpose of the announcement. Therefore, the correct answer is (B).

10. This question tests your comprehension of a radio announcement in standard spoken Spanish. Choice (A) best reflects the purpose of the program, although choices (B), (C), and (D) also fall under the general category of health. Be careful to distinguish between *presión arterial*, mentioned in the selection, and choice (B), *depresión*. The correct answer for this question is (A).

11. This question tests your ability to identify details and make inferences from a listening selection. The radio announcement specifically mentions that the program takes place every Thursday. Therefore, the correct answer is one time per week *(Una vez por semana)*, choice (B).

12. Although choices (A), (B), and (C) are logical ways to gather additional information, they are not mentioned in the ad. The ad does, however, specifically mention calling the office for further information. Therefore, the correct answer is (D).

13. This question tests your comprehension of an announcement in standard spoken Spanish. The selection includes the key words *unir* and *fusión*, which indicate the merger between the two companies. The correct answer, therefore, is choice (B).

14. This question tests your skill in listening for specific information. The announcement begins with: *Si usted es el dueño de una compañía pequeña . . .* , which is a direct reference to choice (C), small-business owners, the correct answer. No direct reference is made to any of the other answer choices.

15. This question tests your ability to understand specific information given over the radio. The announcement suggests taking your last three bills to the office *(lleve sus tres últimas facturas a la oficina)* and also offers office hours. From these pieces of information, the listener can know what to do to receive assistance. The other choices may be logical actions in this situation but are not mentioned in the announcement. The correct answer, therefore, is (B).

16. This question tests your ability to listen to standard spoken Spanish and hear important information of general interest. There is no mention in the commentary about amounts of medication or about research or emergency services. Thus, (A), (B), and (D) cannot be correct answers. The selection does mention that one cannot assume that a child and an adult have the same illness even though the symptoms may be similar. The correct choice, therefore, is (C).

17. This question tests your ability to make inferences from information that is provided in standard spoken Spanish. Although choices (A), (C), and (D) are logical steps a parent might take, they do not reflect what is said in this particular commentary. The narrator counsels against improvised treatment for a sick child *(no improvise en su tratamiento)*, which supports the inference that symptoms should be carefully evaluated *(Tomando en serio cada síntoma)*. The correct answer, therefore, is (B).

18. This question tests your ability to determine the intended audience of a spoken passage. Parents are clearly addressed by the reference to *su hijo* (your child). This reference eliminates choices (A), (B), and (D). The correct answer, therefore, is (C).

19. This question tests your ability to understand spoken Spanish, focusing on specific vocabulary references. Mention of *dominicana* and *Santo Domingo* in the narrative clearly point to the correct answer, (D). Though there are other references to Latin America, specifically *México*, careful listening for detail clearly indicates *la República Dominicana*, as related to *Leonor de Ovando* and *Salomé Ureña*.

20. This question tests listening comprehension skills and attention to fine details. The references in the passage indicate that the two women wrote in different times *(Santo Domingo colonial, se anticipó)* and places *(Santo Domingo, México)*, which make choices (B) and (D) incorrect. There is no reference to themes, which eliminates choice (C). There are several indications that both women were nuns *(una monja, celda de convento, otra religiosa, Sor)*. The correct answer, therefore, is (A).

21. This question tests listening comprehension of important details and your ability to distinguish between related words and their meanings. The passage mentions that *Salomé Ureña* took charge of a historic challenge *(se hizo cargo de un gran reto histórico)*, but there is no reference to teaching history or government work. It also mentions her capacity for work *(capacidad de trabajo)* but nothing about workers. Careful listening and understanding will thus eliminate choices (A), (B), and (D). There is, however, a very clear reference to her work with educational systems *(promocionó el desarrollo cultural de su país, así como su sistema educativo)*. Therefore, the correct answer is (C).

22. This question tests your ability to make inferences from information you hear. There are several references made by both the mother and the teacher that indicate that Carlos is very studious *(saca muy buenas notas, se preocupa mucho por su tarea, es muy buen estudiante)*. No mention is made of athletics, artistic talent, or lack of interest. Therefore, the correct answer is (C).

23. This question tests listening comprehension of main ideas. In the conversation, there are references to grades *(notas)*, homework *(tareas)*, and a university *(una universidad)*, but the reason the mother wants to speak with the teacher is to ask her about a summer program for Carlos *(Un programa de verano para Carlos)*. Therefore, the correct answer is (B).

24. This question tests your ability to listen for details. There are words included in each of the choices that are mentioned in the conversation *(matemáticas, actividades, solicitud)*, but what the teacher advises is that the mother consider what Carlos wants to do *(si Carlos realmente quiere ir, yo le aconsejaría que lo animara; lo más importante es que él quiera participar)*. Therefore, the correct answer is (C).

25. This question tests your knowledge of noun-adjective agreement. The word *luz* is feminine and requires the feminine form of *algún*, which is *alguna*. In choices (A), (B), and (C), all original words are correct *(ayer, algo, o)*; the only choice that indicates a needed revision is (D). The correct answer, therefore, is (D).

26. The question tests your knowledge of the impersonal passive voice in Spanish. In this example, *nada* is the subject and therefore requires *se oye* instead of *se oyen*. Another clue for choosing the correct answer is *se ve*. The correct answer, therefore, is (C).

27. This question tests your knowledge of correct verb tenses in Spanish. There is no indication that the subjunctive of *deber (debamos)* is needed, so a revision is needed for this choice. Based on context there is a need to express probability. Therefore, the conditional *(deberíamos)* is required. The correct answer for this question is (B).

28. This question tests your knowledge of correct use of direct and indirect object pronouns in Spanish. In this sentence, *ayudarlo* uses the third person singular masculine direct object pronoun *(-lo)* when the third person singular <u>indirect</u> object pronoun *(-le)* should be used. Therefore the correct answer for this question is (D).

29. This question tests your knowledge of the correct use of verb tenses in Spanish. Based on the context of the conversation, the tense called for is the present *(tengo)* rather than the preterite *(tuve)*. The correct answer, therefore, is (A).

30. This question tests your knowledge of noun-adjective agreement. The adjective *medio* is referring to the feminine noun *hora* and should appear in the feminine form, *media*. The correct answer, therefore, is (D).

31. This question tests your knowledge of consistency of subject-verb agreement and appropriate register. The conversation has been formal, including the phrase *Usted ha llegado . . . .* The command that follows *(Siéntate)* should also be formal *(Siéntese)*. Therefore, the correct answer is (D).

32. This question tests your knowledge of subject-verb agreement in Spanish. The subject is *ventanas* and calls for the third person plural form, *estaban*, instead of the singular form, *estaba*. All other choices (A), (B), and (D) provide accurate uses of those words. The correct answer, therefore, is (C).

33. This question tests your knowledge of appropriate question words. *Adónde* is used with verbs of motion (e.g., *¿Adónde vas?*). In this case, *dónde* would be the appropriate interrogative word used with the verb *poner (pusiste)*. The correct answer, therefore, is (A).

34. This question tests your knowledge of correct use of verb forms. The context of the passage calls for a conjugated verb, in this case in the imperfect *(quedaban)* to reflect description in the past, not the gerund *(quedando)*. Therefore, the correct answer is (C).

35. This question tests your knowledge of the idiomatic expression *tener* + *que* + infinitive. In this paragraph, the word *que* is omitted. Choice (C) reflects this error. Therefore, the correct answer is (C).

36. This question tests your knowledge of correct word usage. The word *tras* is typically used in sequential expressions (e.g., *día tras día*). In this selection, a better word choice is *atrás*, which would accurately reflect "leaving the city behind." The correct answer, therefore, is (B).

37. This question tests your knowledge of the correct use of *haber* to express "there is/there are" with nouns. The noun *expectativa* ("expectation") would reflect this use in the past ("there was") in the context of this passage and would require *había*. Therefore, *estaba*, although in the correct verb tense, is the incorrect verb to be used. The correct answer choice for this question is (B).

38. This question tests your knowledge of usage of correct verb forms. The conjugated verb *parecían* would have to be followed by an infinitive, *descansar*, rather than a gerund, as might be the case in English. The correct answer, therefore, is (D).

39. This question tests your knowledge of noun-article agreement. The word *puente* is a masculine singular noun and requires the article *el* instead of *la*. The adjective *dañado* would also indicate that *puente* is a masculine noun. The correct answer, therefore, is (B).

40. This question is testing your knowledge of correct word usage. Choice (A), *Atender*, is a false cognate with English. The translation of (B), *Asistir*, is "to attend." The correct answer, therefore, is (B).

41. This question tests your knowledge of Spanish grammar. When a family name is used to refer to more than one person, it is necessary to use the definite article *los* without any change to the last name. Choice (B) does not make sense in the context of the question. Adding the preposition *de* in front of a last name is used by Spanish speakers to indicate a woman's married name (e.g., *María Sánchez de Fernández*), which makes (C) an incorrect choice. Choice (D) is incorrect because one does not pluralize last names in Spanish. The correct answer, therefore, is (A).

42. This question tests your knowledge of changes made to adjectives to reflect noun gender. Choices (A), (B), and (C) do not need to be changed to reflect gender. The adjective *alemán* would need to be changed to *alemana* (note that the accent is lost when the adjective becomes feminine) in order to modify a feminine noun. The correct answer, therefore, is (D).

43. This question tests your knowledge of Spanish grammar. The use of the suffix *-ísimo* indicates an absolute superlative in Spanish. For example, *grandísimo* indicates something extremely large. Choices (A) and (D) are sometimes shown as simple endings to adjectives (e.g., *disponible, amable)* without reference to degree. While choice (C), *-ona,* reflects a greater degree of the adjective, it does not refer to the absolute superlative. The correct answer, therefore, is (B).

44. This question tests your knowledge of idiomatic expressions in Spanish that are used to ask how a person feels. Choices (A), (C), and (D) correspond to different ways of asking that question. Choice (B), however, means "How are you?" not in the sense of "How are you feeling?" but in the sense of "What kind of a person are you?" Therefore, the correct answer is (B).

45. This question tests your knowledge of Spanish grammar. Choices (A) and (B) are incorrect because the novel is not being compared, which the use of *tan* would indicate. Choice (D) is incorrect because *que* would indicate "that which" or a second clause that does not exist. *Lo* with an adverb *(bien)* translates as the English "how"; in this case, "how well written" *(lo bien escrita)*. The correct answer, therefore, is (C).

46. This question tests your knowledge of Spanish grammar and the use of past verb tenses to convey shades of meaning in the past. *Acababa de* + infinitive conveys the meaning of "had just" + past participle, which is the correct meaning in the context of the selection. The correct answer, therefore, is (C).

47. This question tests your knowledge of Spanish grammar and the use of the correct tense of the verb *leer*. Choices (A) and (C) are incorrect because they use the third person plural and the subject is singular *(el profesor)*. Choice (B) *(lea)* is incorrect because there is no need for a formal command or the use of the present subjunctive. Choice (D) accurately conveys the meaning of "had read." The correct answer, therefore, is (D).

48. This question tests your knowledge of correct word choice in context. Choice (A), *fin de que*, means "so that"; choice (B), *menos que*, means "unless"; and choice (D), *manera de*, means "in the form of." None of these adverbial clauses fits the context of the sentence. Choice (C), *pesar de,* conveys "in spite of," which adequately fits the meaning. The correct answer, therefore, is choice (C).

49. This question tests your knowledge of Spanish grammar and the correct tense of the verb *hacer* within the context of the passage. Choice (A), the imperfect tense, would refer to repeatedly making plans. There is no indication that a present subjunctive is needed; therefore, choice (B) is incorrect. Choice (C), the conditional perfect, implies what you would have done (but did not). The passage indicates that the plans had already been made. Choice (D), the pluperfect indicative tense, is therefore the correct answer.

50. This question tests your knowledge of the use of prepositions in certain common idiomatic expressions. English "impossible" + infinitive (e.g., impossible to anticipate) is conveyed in Spanish by *imposible* + *de* + infinitive. The correct answer, therefore, is (A).

51. This question tests reading comprehension skills and recognition of fine details. The passage states the location of the action. In lines 21–22 *(Le molestaba la oscuridad del vasto jardín . . .)*, the author clearly indicates that choice (B) is the right answer. Although there are references that might suggest a park *(rana, ramitas)*, the man is looking into the windows of a house from outside. It is very unlikely that the house is inside a park. There are no references in the passage that should lead the reader to choices (C) and (D). The correct answer, therefore, is (B).

52. This question tests reading comprehension skills and the ability to understand characteristics of main characters. The passage describes several noises that startled the man (e.g., *crujía una ramita, croaba una rana, vibraban los vidrios*). Choices (B) and (D) are mentioned in the passage, but they represent existing conditions. The chandelier *(araña)* was on and gave off light *(luces)*, and the man was looking at it through the window. Choice (A) is incorrect because the child never appears. The correct answer, therefore, is (C).

53. This question tests reading comprehension skills and the ability to make inferences from written materials. In line 6, the phrase *Pero el niño aún no aparecía* implies that the man was waiting for the child to arrive. Choices (A) and (C) are incorrect because the man is never inside the house. Choice (B) is incorrect because no conversation takes place during the passage. The correct answer, therefore, is (D).

54. This question tests your ability to make inferences from written materials. In lines 11–12, the sentence *Había sido corto de vista desde joven* implies that he could not see well and therefore could not see where the shadows were coming from. The correct answer, therefore, is (B).

55. This question tests your ability to derive meaning and make inferences from supporting evidence. In lines 16–17, the statement *Los insectos pululaban, y los manoteos desesperados de don Eulogio . . .* conveys that his gestures *(manoteos)* were caused by the disturbing insects. Therefore, (A) is the correct answer.

56. This question tests your reading comprehension skills and your ability to make inferences from written materials. The passage makes numerous references to the emotional state of *don Eulogio*. For example, *saltaba con agilidad de su asiento; Sacudido por un temblor nervioso*. Although his enthusiasm is mentioned in line 18–19 *(El entusiasmo y la excitación . . .)*, the author clearly states that by the end of the day, this had changed *(habían decaído y sentía ahora cansancio)*. This makes choice (D) incorrect. The correct answer is (A).

57. This question tests your reading comprehension skills and the ability to make inferences from written materials. Lines 4–5 *(Era la época de la revolución mexicana y mi padre, que había participado en política . . .)* clearly imply that the father had had to flee *(tuvo que salir huyendo)* because of his association with the political leader, Emiliano Zapata. The correct answer, therefore, is (B).

58. This question tests your reading comprehension skills and ability to make inferences from written materials. Choice (C) is incorrect because Octavio Paz met his father at the border. Careful reading of lines 14–16 show why choices (A) and (B) are incorrect and indicate that the trip was difficult and dangerous and lasted more than a week. The correct answer, therefore, is (D).

59. This question tests reading comprehension skills and the ability to make inferences from written materials. Although choices (A), (C), and (D) may be logical responses, they are not mentioned in the passage. Lines 19–22 and 32–35 state that Octavio Paz believed that learning another language was enriching and allowed for deeper poetic descriptions. The correct answer, therefore, is (B).

60. This question tests your reading comprehension skills and the ability to recognize important details in written passages. In lines 33–34 (. . . *que es maravilloso que los mismos objetos tengan nombres distintos . . .*), Octavio Paz expresses his opinion about the advantage of knowing a second language. The correct answer, therefore, is (C).

61. This question tests reading comprehension skills and the ability to make inferences from written materials. In lines 41–43 (. . . *escribí mucho sobre México porque México se convirtió en una pasión, en una pasión doble . . .*), Octavio Paz describes his feelings for his homeland. It became a passion possible only by leaving Mexico (. . . *no hubiera sido posible sin estas ausencias*). The correct answer, therefore, is (A).

62. This question tests reading comprehension skills and the ability to recognize important details in written passages. Choices (A), (B), and (D) are never referred to in the passage. Lines 46–47 state that *Los españoles viajaron mucho; cuando dejaron de viajar, escribieron menos bien.* This implies that the opportunity to travel opens new doors for an author and helps the person to become a better writer. The correct answer, therefore, is (C).

63. This question tests your reading comprehension skills to determine the main facts in a passage. Choice (A) is clearly stated in lines 2–3 (*buscando una niña que pudiera interpretar un papel . . .*). The correct answer, therefore, is (A).

64. This question tests your reading comprehension skills and ability to determine important facts in a passage. In lines 7–8, the author states *Ella ni siquiera se acuerda de aquel encuentro. Era demasiado pequeña.* This indicates that she was too young to remember (note that *"pequeña"* refers to age, not size, in this case). The correct answer, therefore, is (D).

65. This question tests your reading comprehension skills and ability to interpret descriptions. Lines 8–9 mention that Erice is unable to forget the face of Ana Torrent. The passage also mentions her innocent and expressive eyes (*esos ojos inocentes y expresivos*). Since *rostro* is a synonym for *cara,* choice (C) is the correct answer.

66. This question tests your ability to make inferences. Choices (B), (C), and (D) can be eliminated because no mention is ever made of any of these situations. In lines 16–22, Ana discusses her lack of formal training. The correct answer, therefore, is (A).

67. This question tests your ability to make inferences. In lines 28–29, the author refers to the father's efforts to protect his daughter (*Su padre procuró por todos los medios que aquella aventura no le afectara . . .*) and gives an example of how the father even rejected a role for her (*se negó*). An additional example is in lines 35–37, where Ana herself talks about her father's worries (. . . *mi padre tenía miedo de que me convirtiera en la típica niña de cine . . .*). All of these examples support the father's concern that Ana's work might harm her (*perjudicar*). The correct answer, therefore, is (A).

68. This question tests your reading comprehension skills and ability to follow the chronology of written material. Ana's feelings regarding choices (A), (C), and (D) are never mentioned. In line 41–42, the expression *le daba exactamente igual* indicates her indifference toward the second film. Therefore, the correct answer is (B).

69. This question tests your ability to identify the main idea of a passage. The text reviews the progression of Marina Mayoral's literary career. Although choice (A) might be attractive because Mayoral wrote short stories, within the passage there is no study of a specific story. Choices (B) and (D) are mentioned, but they are not the primary focus of the passage. The selection discusses the varied nature of influences on her texts, therefore providing a review of her literary contributions. The correct answer is (C).

70. This question tests your ability to recognize important details within a reading passage. The author clearly states that Mayoral broke away from other styles of literature (*una ruptura con varias tradiciones literarias*), listing several movements, including the *Generación del '98*. The correct answer, therefore, is (B).

71. This question also tests your ability to identify important information. The author states that *Mayoral pide prestados elementos de los géneros populares* and *Es una lectura amena por los elementos populares que introduce*. These are positive statements of the influence of popular genres on Mayoral's work. The correct answer, therefore, is (B).

72. This question tests your ability to make inferences. The text states that *Mayoral pide prestado elementos de los géneros populares como la novela rosa y la novela policíaca para atraer al lector*. These two genres inspired Mayoral's work. The correct answer, therefore, is (A).

73. This question tests your ability to summarize ideas. Lines 34–35 state that *Mayoral cree que el cuento es un género literario injustamente despreciado*. Since *despreciado* is a synonym for *inapreciado*, the correct answer is (A).

74. This question tests your ability to make inferences based on careful reading of the text. The passage indicates that the primary requirement of all narration is to tell a story that interests the reader (*al primer requisito de toda narración—contar una historia que interese al lector*), therefore, reflecting the most important objective (*objetivo primordial*) of writers. Although choices (A), (B), and (C) are mentioned in the passage, they are characteristics of Mayoral's writing, not primary objectives of narration. Therefore, the correct answer is (D).

75. This question tests your knowledge of Mexican history. The name of Emiliano Zapata is associated with the Mexican Revolution of 1910. Therefore, the correct answer is (A).

76. This question tests your knowledge of Hispanic artists. In choice (B), Picasso and Miró were artists from Spain. In choice (C), El Greco was born in Greece but established himself in Spain; de Goya was Spanish. Both were court painters. In choice (D), Dalí was from Spain and Botero is from Colombia. In choice (A), both Kahlo and Rivera were of Mexican origin. The correct answer, therefore, is (A).

77. This question tests your knowledge of major literary works in Spanish. Choice (A), written by Miguel de Cervantes, was published in two parts in 1605 and 1615. It was a *novela de caballería*. Choice (B), written by Gabriel García Márquez, was published in 1967 and is one of the best examples of *el realismo mágico*. Choice (C), written by Ricardo Güiraldes, was published in 1926 and is considered one of the finest examples of the *novela gauchesca*. Choice (D), written anonymously in the sixteenth century, was the first *novela picaresca*. Therefore, the correct answer is (D).

78. This question tests your knowledge of the history of indigenous civilizations and cultures. Choice (A), *Los olmecas*, represents a civilization that inhabited the area of Mexico now known as Veracruz from 1500 B.C.E. Choice (B), *Los aztecas,* is the name given to a civilization that thrived in what is now southern Mexico. Choice (D), *Los mayas,* was the most advanced civilization of Mesoamerica. They are associated with the region that is today Mexico, Guatemala, Honduras, and the coast of El Salvador. The Inca civilization was established around C.E. 1100 in the area of Peru known as Cuzco. The correct answer, therefore, is (C).

79. This question tests your knowledge of Spanish history and geography. The Moors invaded Spain in 711. They invaded the southern area of the peninsula, now known as the region of Andalucía, which included Córdoba, Granada, and Sevilla. Defeat of the Moorish army put an end to their expansion into northern Spain, although Andalucía remained under Muslim rule until 1492. Barcelona is located in the northeastern part of Spain. The correct answer, therefore, is (D).

80. This question tests your knowledge of traditional celebrations in some parts of Latin America and Spain. The selection is an invitation to a *quinceañera*, a celebration of a girl's fifteenth birthday. The correct answer, therefore, is (C).

81. This question tests your knowledge of key political figures in the Hispanic world. Choice (A), Porfirio Díaz, is associated with Mexican history. Choice (B), Simón Bolívar, is associated with the independence of various South American countries, mostly in the northern part (known at the time as *Gran Colombia*, which included what is now Venezuela, Colombia, and parts of Ecuador and Peru). Choice (C), Fulgencio Batista, was president of Cuba when Fidel Castro seized power. José de San Martín was a key figure in Argentina's independence. The correct answer, therefore, is (D).

82. This question tests your cultural knowledge of regional vocabulary associated with food. Choice (A), *las onces*, is a snack eaten at 11:00 in the morning in some Latin American countries. Choices (C) and (D) are general terms shared in most Spanish-speaking countries to refer to food or a meal *(la comida)* and snacks *(las meriendas)*. *Las tapas* are consumed in Spain (although they have become popular in other parts of the world) in the afternoon and evening. The correct answer, therefore, is (B).

83. This question tests your knowledge of geography. Choices (A), (B), and (C) all have coastlines on the Caribbean Sea: Puerto Rico, the Dominican Republic, and Mexico, respectively. Palma de Mallorca, however, is located in Spain on the Mediterranean Sea coast. Therefore, the correct answer is (D).

84. This question tests your knowledge of the location of various countries in South America and some of their geographical characteristics. *El Río de la Plata* runs between Argentina and Uruguay, which are numbered 7 and 9 on the map. The correct answer, therefore, is (D).

85. This question tests your knowledge of geography and important archaeological sites. Machu Picchu is located in Peru, which is numbered 4 on the map. The correct answer, therefore, is (B).

86. This question tests your knowledge of historic and literary figures. José Martí is a famous nineteenth-century Cuban writer (*Versos sencillos* and *La edad de oro* are two of his better-known works) and a patriot who fought for the freedom of his country from Spain. The correct answer, therefore, is (C).

87. This question tests your knowledge of geography and important cities. All the cities referred to are located in Mexico. The correct answer, therefore, is (A).

88. This question tests your knowledge of culture and Latin American figures. Since all the people mentioned were writers, the only logical choice is that they were recipients of the Nobel Prize in Literature. The correct answer, therefore, is (A).

89. This question tests your knowledge of the history and culture of Spain. The examples provided are both linked to the Arabic influence in Spain. The correct answer, therefore, is (C).

90. This question tests your knowledge of Latin American dances. Choice (A), *El bolero*, is associated with Cuba and the Caribbean region. Choice (B), *La samba*, is a product of Brazil. Choice (C), *El tango*, had its origins in Argentina. Choice (D), *El merengue*, originated in the Dominican Republic. Thus, the correct answer is (C).

Chapter 7

Preparing for *Spanish: Productive Language Skills*

▶ ▶ ▶ ▶ ▶ ▶ ▶ ▶ ▶ ▶ ▶ ▶

The purpose of this chapter is to provide you with strategies for listening to, reading carefully, and understanding the questions on the Praxis *Spanish: Productive Language Skills (PLS)* test in order for you to be able to provide proficient oral and written responses in Spanish.

Introduction to the Test

The test is designed for candidates applying for licenses or credentials to teach Spanish in grades K-12. The Praxis *Spanish: PLS* test measures the speaking and writing proficiency of prospective teachers of Spanish. The test questions elicit samples of speaking and writing skills that a teacher of Spanish needs in order to demonstrate the language in the classroom clearly and accurately and to develop and improve students' performance in all four language skills: listening, speaking, reading, and writing. This test is designed to gather evidence about your knowledge of the Spanish language and your ability to use it.

The test contains a total of nine questions:

- Six questions consist of stimuli or situations to which you must provide spoken responses in Spanish.

- Three questions consist of stimuli or situations to which you must provide written responses in Spanish.

In all nine questions, you will have to demonstrate that you can correctly use various verb tenses and moods, express ideas, and describe situations accurately and fluently. Your response must demonstrate an appropriate range of vocabulary and idioms for the task presented in each question.

What to Study

Success on this test is not simply a matter of learning more about how to respond to the question types on the test; it also takes real knowledge of Spanish language and culture. You must show the ability to produce comprehensible and proficient oral or written responses to each question. It must be obvious that your ability in all four language skills (reading, listening, speaking, and writing) in Spanish is strong enough to serve as a solid, desirable model in guiding your students in the classroom to develop and improve their own capabilities in the Spanish language.

Therefore, it would serve you well to consider the following areas for review prior to taking the test.

1. Familiarize yourself with the test content and format by reviewing this chapter and taking the practice test included in this study guide.

2. Review the chapter containing sample responses to the practice test and explanations for how the responses were scored. Compare your responses to the high-scoring responses in this chapter to develop a sense of areas in which you need further review and practice. Then, refer to additional resources to help you brush up on those areas.

Depending on your Spanish-language skills, you may find the following materials helpful.

AP Spanish: Preparing for the Language Examination. Diaz, José M., Margarita Leicher-Prieto, and Glenn J. Nadelbach. White Plains, NY: Longman, 1996.

Composición práctica: Conversación y repaso. González, Trinidad, and Joseph Farrell. New York: Wiley, 2001.

Conversation in Spanish: Points of Departure. Sedwick, Frank. New York: Van Nostrand, 2002.

Dos mundos: A Communicative Approach. 5th ed. Terrell, Tracy, Magdalena Andrade, Jeanne Egasse, and Elías Miguel Muñoz. Boston: McGraw-Hill, 2002.

Essential Repaso: A Complete Review of Spanish Grammar, Communication, and Culture. Lincolnwood, IL: National Textbook Company, 1998.

Repase y escriba: Curso avanzado de gramática y composición. Dominicis, Maria Canteli, and John J. Reynolds. Saddle Brook, NJ: Wiley, 2003.

Spanish Composition through Literature. 4th ed. Ayllón, Cándido, Paul Smith, and Antonio Morillo. Upper Saddle River, NJ: Prentice-Hall, 2002.

Workbook in Spanish, Three Years. Nassi, Robert J., Bernard Bernstein, and Theodore F. Nuzzi. New York: Amsco School Publications, Inc., 1989.

The above-mentioned materials are particularly relevant to the types of knowledge, topics, and skills covered on the test. Note, however, that the test is not based on these resources. Instead, the list of works is intended to help you revisit topics you have already covered in your Spanish courses.

Understanding What the Questions Are Asking

It is impossible to produce orally, or in written form, a successful response to a question unless you thoroughly understand the question. Test takers often jump into a response without taking enough time to understand exactly what the question is asking, how different parts of the question need to be addressed, and how the information in the written prompts and picture stimuli need to be approached and used. The appropriate time and attention you invest in making sure you understand what the question is asking will definitely pay off in a better performance. Examine the overall question closely; then identify what specific information and details your response should contain.

In the preparation time allotted for each question, mentally organize your response and take notes in the space provided in your test book. Write down key words and outline your answer. Leave yourself plenty of time to speak or write your answer.

Speaking Section Question Types

To illustrate the importance of understanding the question before you begin answering, let's look at the question types for the Presentational Speaking section:

1. Role-playing/Phone message

This question type describes a situation that requires you to request a favor from someone in order to solve a problem. Listen to and read the description of the situation carefully. You should outline your answer by writing down key words and brief notes to guide your spoken response. Make sure that you clearly and precisely address each of the information items you are required to include in your answer.

2. Picture description

This question type presents a picture of an everyday scene, which usually shows an incident in progress. For a good response, you should demonstrate the ability to use different verb tenses and moods, such as present, past, future, and conditional. Make sure that, once again, you clearly address each prompt or task that accompanies the picture. Someone who cannot see the picture must be able to visualize it from the detailed description of your response.

Prior to taking the test, you might want to practice key verbs in major tenses by describing an interesting picture from a magazine. Within a two-minute period, explain in Spanish what has just happened, what is happening now, what people would probably say, what will most likely happen next, and how the incident could have been avoided.

3. Giving instructions or giving a narration of a series of pictures

In this question, you are required to give instructions (using the imperative) or tell a story (using past tenses) describing a progression of activities. A sequence of six to nine pictures is provided to assist you in formulating your response. The necessary vocabulary can be fairly specific. It is imperative that you say something about each picture in the logical sequence. Do not try to lump two or more pictures together in your description. Don't forget that you are speaking to someone who cannot see the pictures you are describing. Scorers advise that examinees use appropriate verb tenses and do not elaborate into areas that are not illustrated in the pictures. Stay on task.

4. Stating and defending an opinion

In this question type, you must carefully use the allotted preparation time to take notes and outline the presentation of your opinion. Jot down key vocabulary words that you will use to support as many specific examples as possible in defense of your opinion. Clarity in stating your point of view is critical and should be immediately apparent in the introduction of your response. You then should give, in an orderly fashion, detailed examples that clearly address and support the objectives of your answer, for or against the idea.

5. Oral paraphrase

First, it is assumed by scorers that you fully understand what "paraphrase" means. If you are uncertain, the *New Oxford American Dictionary* definition is "rewording or restating the meaning of a spoken or written passage using different words (if possible) to achieve greater clarity." In this question, you will hear a passage read twice, during which time you have the opportunity to take notes while listening. You will be required to retell the story in Spanish. You must demonstrate your listening comprehension skills to produce an accurate recreation of the passage with appropriate vocabulary. You do not translate, analyze, or critique the passage; you simply restate the contents of the passage. It need not be word for word; it can be in your own words, but your paraphrase must contain all the essential points of the story, including the ending, which at times may reveal a surprise conclusion. The keys to a good response are accuracy and completion.

6. Brief talk

This question type requires that you prepare and deliver a short, formal talk to a particular gathering of people. The directions establish the premise of a determined situation. The prompts for this question usually have two parts: (1) greetings, thanks, and acknowledgement of the situation and (2) substantial, detailed information about the purpose or intended results of the situation. This second part should make up the greater portion of your response. Listen to and read very carefully what specific information is expected in the content of your speech. Outline your talk with key words and details so your delivery will flow smoothly, with a minimum of hesitation and the proper degree of formality, which is especially important for this talk.

Writing Section Question Types

It is obvious and quite natural that errors will show up much more clearly in a written response than in a spoken one. Inappropriate or limited vocabulary and idiomatic expressions, wrong word order, accent marks, spelling, and, most of all, poor grammatical control are all quickly exposed in written responses.

Common errors in standard written Spanish include the following:

- The contractions *al* and *del*
- Subject-verb agreement errors
- Misuse of past tenses, particularly the preterite and imperfect
- Misusing and confusing direct and indirect object pronouns
- Poor use of, or missing, connectors and prepositions
- Wrong gender
- Wrong word order
- Missing or inaccurately placed accents
- "Anglicisms": American syntax, vocabulary, and idiomatic expressions transcribed into Spanish word for word

To illustrate the importance of understanding the question before you begin answering, let's look at the question types for the Presentational Writing section.

7. Picture narration

This question type presents a series of pictures (usually six) for which you must write a continuous narrative. There is always a lead-in prompt that clearly suggests the use of past tenses. *"La semana pasada . . ."* is a common example. Therefore, scorers will expect at least the appropriate, simultaneous use of the preterite and imperfect tenses. Do not deviate from what is in the pictures. Make sure to write something about each picture and keep the narrative flowing. Do not assume that the reader can see the pictures.

8. Writing a letter or e-mail

You may wish to practice writing a formal letter or e-mail at home before taking the actual test. Check out samples of formal or business letters in a university-level grammar/composition textbook. Possibilities are a business letter to a store or company concerning purchase of merchandise, or a cover letter for a job application. Be aware of the specific types of opening and closing salutations in Spanish. The directions and prompts for this type of question are very specific. Include information requested in each of the prompt items in the order provided. These prompts will very likely suggest the use of various verb tenses (e.g., past, future, conditional, subjunctive) and specialized vocabulary. Communicating formally in writing requires that you not use the *tú* form in addressing people but, rather, *usted*.

9. Writing questions

Here, in response to a particular situation described in the test book, you are required to write four questions addressed to one or more persons. The situation could relate to one person you are expected to interview, for example. The four questions should be very clear and deal only with the subject presented in the prompt. One can be a short-answer question; the other three questions should extract longer answers, such as an opinion, a description, or a narration. You may ask a two-part question, but do not combine several questions into one question. Do not ask silly, personal, or insensitive questions, such as "What is your name? Are you divorced/married?" Maintain a proper degree of politeness and formality. Never use the *tú* form; always use *usted*. Your complete written response will involve a relatively small amount of text, so individual errors may be costly; your grammar, sentence-construction, and spelling mistakes will count a great deal in determining your score. Check your questions carefully after you have finished. You may wish to practice at home prior to taking the test. For example, assume that you are writing four questions that you will ask an exchange Spanish teacher who has just arrived at your school.

How the Test Scorers Evaluate Your Responses

Even if you feel confident about your language skills and knowledge of the content to be tested, you still may want to know how the scorers evaluate your answers. The fact is that you can find out what the test scorers want by looking carefully at the questions themselves. The Praxis *Spanish: PLS* test questions are worded as clearly as possible regarding the specific tasks you are expected to do. The Spanish educators who evaluate your responses base your score on two considerations:

■ whether you do all the tasks that the question requests

■ how well you do them using the Spanish language skills you possess

The *Spanish: PLS* test is scored by expert teachers of Spanish from high schools, community colleges, and universities, educators who have many years of experience scoring Praxis Spanish tests. The team of scorers/readers is made up of both native and nonnative speakers of Spanish, representative of diverse personal backgrounds. Scorers follow strict procedures to ensure that scoring is fair and consistent. Scores are based on carefully established criteria in the scoring guide; they do not reflect the scorers' personal opinions or preferences. At the readings, or scoring sessions, the process involves a number of critical steps to confirm the quality of the scoring process.

■ All scorers, whether they are long-experienced readers or not, undergo rigorous training before and during the scoring session.

■ The scoring guide is completely reviewed and studied so everyone clearly understands the criteria for each score (ranging from 0 to 4).

■ Old benchmark responses are used prior to the actual scoring to illustrate how the criteria determine each of the scores of 0 to 4 for each question.

■ During the actual scoring of your test, each question is scored twice, once each by two different readers working independently. The two scores for a given question must never be more than one point apart. Scores that are more than one point apart represent a discrepancy, which is immediately resolved by the scoring leader, who scores the response a third time. This step reinforces strict adherence to the criteria set in the scoring guide.

■ The scorers' performances are continuously monitored by the scoring leader to keep everyone focused on the consistent and accurate application of the scoring criteria.

■ The *Spanish: PLS* test is scored holistically. Scorers first assess the quality and overall comprehensibility of the response. The four key factors in the criteria that make a difference between one score and another (e.g., between 2 and 3) are as follows:

1. *Comprehensibility.* How much of an effort does the scorer have to make to understand what is being said or written?

2. *Accuracy of content.* Each task of every question must be addressed appropriately and accurately.

3. *Grammatical control.* Strong grammatical control of basic structures that are used with high frequency by speakers and writers in ordinary situations or by teachers of Spanish in a classroom, is essential for scores of 3 and 4.

4. *Fluency.* Spoken and written fluency should demonstrate control of complex sentences, connectors, and transition words, and some elaboration to give substance to a response. A response made up of single words or short, choppy phrases, poorly formulated sentences, limited vocabulary with little or no idiomatic constructions, and no elaboration will very likely score a 2.

Sample Questions

To answer more specifically the question, "How do the scorers evaluate your responses?" we should look at sample questions much like the ones you will encounter on the test.

Picture Description—Speaking

Directions: In this question, you are asked to describe in Spanish the picture in your test book. Do <u>not</u> assume that the person listening can see the picture. In your description, include <u>all</u> of the following details:

- A description of where this incident is taking place;

- What has just occurred;

- What the woman probably would say to the man in this situation;

- What is probably going to happen next;

- How this situation could have been avoided.

Before you are asked to speak, you will have <u>2 minutes</u> to study the picture and think about your response. Then you will have <u>2 minutes</u> to give your response.

Reading the Question—Key Components of the Question

Just focus on understanding the question: what are the parts of the question, and what does each part ask? Here, you are to give a description of the picture and to provide *details for each of the five tasks*, which tell you in general terms what your response should address.

Organizing Your Response

A successful response starts with successful planning, either with an outline or with another form of notes. By planning your response, you greatly decrease the chances that you will forget to answer any part of the question. You increase the chances of creating a well-organized response, which is something the scorers look for.

To illustrate a possible strategy for planning a response, let us focus again on this sample picture-description question. By analyzing the question, we find that it asks for five tasks to be addressed. You might begin by numbering those parts on your notes page, leaving space under each. This will ensure that you address each part when you begin speaking.

First, look at the picture carefully and remember that you are to describe what is happening, not what the people were doing before, or your opinion of their personal relationship. Then jot down key vocabulary words for the objects and actions involved in this incident. Decide which verb tenses you are expected to use for each of the five tasks required.

Sample Notes

Here, you start by identifying each part of the question by quickly writing down the main vocabulary and verb tenses you want to address in each part. Your notes could include some of the following:

1. sala, sala de estar, hombre y mujer, estante, libros, bujerías, plantas, sillón
2. poner [o colocar] un libro en el estante, resbalarse, deslizarse
3. mujer, probablemente, decir, tener cuidado, torpe
4. libros, caerse, bujerías, romperse, al suelo, sorprenderse
5. evitar, atar, clavar, pared, equilibrar

You have now created the skeleton of your oral response and have enough vocabulary to choose from to provide information for each task.

Speaking Your Response

Now the important step of *speaking* your response begins. The scorers will not consider your notes when they score your response, so it is crucial that you integrate all the important ideas from your notes into your actual oral response.

Sample Response (Transcribed with Mistakes) That Earned a Score of 4

Keep in mind that your response need not be perfect to earn a score of 4. There may be some small mistakes, but your oral response must be completely comprehensible, even to a native speaker of Spanish who is not accustomed to dealing with nonnative learners of the language. It must be completely accurate, with appropriate elaboration, strong grammatical control, and broad, precise vocabulary. Your overall fluency should rarely be hesitant, and your pronunciation may be slightly nonnative but always easily comprehensible. *Speak clearly and loudly into your microphone.*

> Este incidente tiene lugar en casa, en la sala de estar de los señores García. La señora García está sentada en un sillón leyendo un libro, y el señor García está en pie delante de un mueble y un estante de libros. Hay unas plantas y otras cosas como un caballito y una foto.
>
> El señor García acaba de colocar un libro al final del estante más alto, a la extrema derecha. Los libros empiezan a resbalarse hacia la derecha, porque el señor García acaba de inclinar el estante en ese sentido.
>
> La mujer diría probablemente a su marido: "Ten cuidado, vas a hacer caer el estante; has puesto demasiados libros en la parte derecha."
>
> Es probable que se caigan todos los libros al suelo junto con el Sr. García. Puede que el estante se rompa y también el caballito y las plantas. Y después habrá que recoger todas las cosas rotas del suelo.
>
> Se habría podido evitar esta situación si el Sr. García hubiera prestado más atención a lo que hacía antes de colocar otro libro en un estante ya sobrecargado, si hubiera puesto los libros en la mitad del estante y si hubiera atado mejor el estante a la pared.

Commentary on Sample Response That Earned a Score of 4

The response is complete and very comprehensible. All five parts of the prompt have been addressed with some elaboration. It would be quite easy to recreate this picture from the description given. The verb tenses are correctly used and show very good grammatical control. Overall, the response demonstrates an excellent knowledge of the language and a full understanding of all parts of the question.

Picture Narration—Writing

Directions: In this question, you are asked to write a <u>continuous</u> story in Spanish, based only on the six pictures below. In your story, tell what happened in <u>each</u> of the six pictures. Do not assume that the reader of the story can see the pictures.

Start the story with the words *"La semana pasada . . . "*

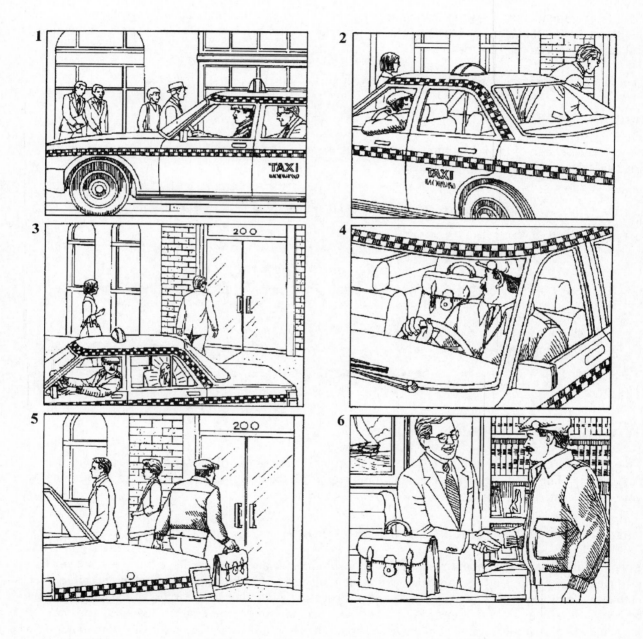

Reading the Question—Key Components of the Question

Focus on the content of the six pictures for which you will have to write a continuous story based solely on the pictures. Your story should be written in the past tense because the prompt tells you to start with *"La semana pasada . . . "* ("Last week . . . ").

Organizing Your Response

First, look at the pictures carefully. Remember that you are to tell something about each picture in order to describe an event that happened "last week." In your notes, jot down key vocabulary words for the objects and actions involved in this story.

The Spanish verb tenses you are likely to use are preterite, imperfect, and pluperfect.

Sample Notes

Your notes for each of the six pictures might include some of the following words and verbs, depending on your knowledge of the Spanish language:

1. taxi, taxista, hombre de negocios, pararse, edificio, peatones
2. de negocios, bajar del taxi
3. edificio, número 200, mirar hacia la izquierda, poner en marcha el taxi asiento de atrás, dejar, maletín, hombre de negocios, dirigirse
4. taxista, mirar hacia atrás, fijarse en, haber olvidado, maletín o cartera grande
5. pararse el taxi, bajar, llevar el maletín
6. encontrar la oficina del hombre de negocios, devolver el maletín, darle las gracias, darle la mano, estar contento, honrado, sonreírse

Writing Your Response

Now the important step of writing your response begins. The scorers will not consider your notes in determining your score, so it is crucial that you integrate all the details of the pictures from your notes into your actual written response.

Sample Response That Earned a Score of 4

Keep in mind that your response need not be perfect to receive a score of 4. There may be some small mistakes (like spelling and accents), but your written response must be completely comprehensible, even to a native speaker of Spanish who is not accustomed to dealing with nonnative learners of the language. It must be completely accurate, with appropriate elaboration, strong grammatical control, and broad, precise vocabulary. Your word choice should be generally idiomatic, rarely awkward, and easily comprehensible.

1. La semana pasada, un hombre de negocios, el Sr. Alonso, fue en taxi a su oficina. El taxi se para delante de un edificio, y hay varios peatones por la acera.
2. El Sr. Alonso se baja del taxi.
3. El hombre de negocios entró en el edificio número 200. Llevaba papeles en la mano. El taxista miró a la izquierda antes de ponerse en marcha. En el asiento de atrás estaba el maletín del Sr. Alonso.
4. Al salir, el taxista miró hacia atrás en el taxi y notó que su pasajero había dejado su maletín en el asiento.
5. El taxista se estacionó delante del número 200. Salió del taxi llevando el maletín del Sr. Alonso.
6. El taxista encontró la oficina del Sr. Alonso y le devolvió su maletín. Este está contento y se sonríe. Da las gracias al taxista por ser hombre honrado y le da la mano. Es probable que le diera otra propina también.

Commentary on Sample Response That Earned a Score of 4

The response is complete and very comprehensible. All six pictures have been described with some elaboration. It would be quite easy to recreate these pictures from the description given. The verb tenses are correctly used and show very good grammatical control. Overall, the response demonstrates an excellent knowledge of the language and a full understanding of the sequence of events in the six pictures, resulting in an accurate story.

Sample Response That Earned a Score of 2

A score of 2 definitely suggests lack of proficiency. Even a sympathetic reader must make an effort to understand and interpret the intended meaning of the response. The grammar and vocabulary are limited, and word choice is often unidiomatic. The response, which is often missing some of the tasks, is poorly organized and not very coherent.

1. La semana pasada, señor Alonso cogo un taxi al trabajo. El señor de el taxi para delante el office de el Sr. Alonso.
2-3. El Sr. Alonso va al office en la puerta 200.
4. El hombre del taxi ha mirado el saco detras el taxi.
5. El señor Alonso olvidaba el saco y el hombre lo lleva el saco.
6. En la oficina el Sr. Alonso toma el saco y gracias al hombre de el taxi.

Commentary on Sample Response That Earned a Score of 2

It is obvious that this response is quite poorly written. There are mistakes throughout. There is no consistency in the use of the past tenses; vocabulary is indeed limited, some of it being direct transpositions of English words, like "office" for *oficina* or *despacho*. Missing accents and contractions and wrong object pronouns also contribute to a poor response. The pictures are poorly described, and it would be somewhat difficult to recreate them just from this written effort.

In Conclusion

The important thing is that your answers be clearly comprehensible, complete, and detailed. You need to be certain to do the following:

- Answer all parts of the question.

- Select appropriate vocabulary and grammatical constructions.

- Demonstrate language-specific knowledge and proficiency in your answer.

- Refer to the data in the stimulus: pictures, written prompts, and directions.

Even though you may be teaching first-year Spanish now, your daily experiences in teaching beginning students are not enough to prepare you adequately to take this test. You need to practice and be exposed to a more advanced level than first-year Spanish. Facility with basic verb tenses is critical not only in teaching students to speak and write Spanish but also in successfully demonstrating in this test that you have a thorough knowledge of basic and advanced Spanish verb forms. Develop your vocabulary by reading different types of materials, fiction and nonfiction. Talk to Spanish-speaking friends whenever you can; listen to the language in films and on cable television, if possible.

It is highly recommended that you use the practice test provided in chapter 9 to help you develop a plan for taking the Praxis *Spanish: PLS* test on the actual testing day.

Chapter 8
Succeeding on Constructed-Response Questions

▶   ▶   ▶   ▶   ▶   ▶   ▶   ▶   ▶   ▶   ▶   ▶

This chapter provides advice for maximizing your success on the *Spanish: Productive Language Skills* test, with special focus on the scoring guides and procedures used by the scorers. Chapter 7 offers step-by-step strategies for working through questions, lists of the topics covered, and lists of sources you can use to prepare.

TIP Advice from the Experts

Scorers who have scored hundreds of real tests were asked to give advice to teacher candidates planning to take the *Spanish: Productive Language Skills* test. The scorers' advice boiled down to the practical suggestions given below.

1. **Read and answer the question accurately.** Be sure to dissect the parts of the question and analyze what each part is asking you to do. If the question asks you to *describe* or *discuss*, keep those requirements in mind when composing your response—do not just give a list.

2. **Answer everything that is asked in the question.** This seems simple, but many test takers fail to provide complete responses. If a question asks you to do three distinct things in your response, don't give a response to just two of those things. No matter how well you speak or write about those two things, the scorers will not award you full credit.

3. **Give a thorough and detailed response.** Your response must indicate to the scorers that you have a thorough command of the Spanish language. The scorers will not read into your response any information that is not specifically stated. If something is not written or spoken, they do not know that you know it and will not give you credit for it.

    A word of caution: Superfluous writing or speaking will obscure your points and will make it difficult for the scorers to be confident of your full understanding of the material. Be straightforward in your response. Do not try to impress the scorers. If you do not know the answer, you cannot receive full credit, but if you do know the answer, provide enough information to convince the scorers that you have a full understanding of what is being asked.

4. **Do not change the question or challenge the basis of the question.** Stay focused on the question that is asked. You will receive no credit or, at best, a low score if you choose to answer another question or if you state, for example, that there is no possible answer. Answer the question by addressing the fundamental topic at hand. Do not venture off topic, for example, to demonstrate your command of vocabulary that is not specifically related to the question. This undermines the impression that you understand the topic adequately.

5. **Reread your written response, both to improve your writing and to check that you have written what you thought you wrote.** Frequently, sentences are left unfinished or clarifying information is omitted.

General Scoring Guides for the *Spanish: Productive Language Skills* Test

The scorers' advice corresponds with the official scoring criteria used at scoring sessions. It is a good idea to be familiar with the scoring rubrics so you can maximize your success and spend your time on things that matter (e.g., demonstrating understanding of the prompts and providing good examples) rather than spending time on things that don't matter (e.g., writing a very long narration or letter).

The following scoring rubrics provide the overarching framework for scoring the questions in the *Spanish: Productive Language Skills* test.

Each question on the test is scored on a scale from 0 to 4. The response is considered in its entirety when the scorer assigns the score.

General Scoring Guides for the *Spanish: Productive Language Skills* Test

Presentational Speaking Section

This scoring guide is used to evaluate responses in the Presentational Speaking section. The score range is 0 to 4.

4
- Is completely and easily comprehensible, even to an unsympathetic listener[1]
- Gives a complete and entirely accurate, relevant response, with appropriate elaboration, to all (or almost all) parts of the question
- May make sporadic errors, but they rarely or never interfere with communication
  - has strong grammatical control (no errors in basic, high-frequency structures; few errors in complex, low-frequency structures; no marked error patterns)
  - employs a broad, precise vocabulary adequate for almost all topics, with word choice that is generally idiomatic and varied and rarely awkward
  - has overall fluency: speech is occasionally or rarely hesitant, with frequent use of complex sentences and "connectors" when appropriate or required
  - may have a slightly nonnative pronunciation, with few or no phonological errors and no error patterns, but is always comprehensible

3
- Is generally comprehensible, even to an unsympathetic listener, but occasionally requires the listener's effort and interpretation of the intended meaning
- Gives a mostly accurate, relevant response to most parts of the question
- Is likely to make errors and/or produce error patterns, but they only occasionally interfere with communication
  - has moderate grammatical control (few errors in basic, high-frequency structures; some errors and/or error patterns in complex, low-frequency structures)
  - employs vocabulary adequate for most general topics, with word choice that is often idiomatic but occasionally awkward
  - has considerable fluency: speech is sometimes hesitant, with some use of complex sentences and "connectors" when appropriate or required
  - may have a markedly nonnative pronunciation with some phonological errors and/or error patterns, but is nearly or always comprehensible

---

[1] "Unsympathetic listener" refers to a native speaker of the language who is NOT accustomed to dealing with nonnative learners of the language. An unsympathetic listener does not make any special effort to understand the test taker.

2
- Is somewhat comprehensible to a sympathetic listener[2], but often requires the listener's effort and interpretation of the intended meaning
- Gives a somewhat accurate, relevant response to some parts of the question
- Produces errors and/or error patterns that may often interfere with communication
    - has limited grammatical control (many errors and/or error patterns in basic, high-frequency structures; no control of complex, low-frequency structures)
    - employs a limited vocabulary, with word choice that is often unidiomatic and awkward
    - has limited fluency, with halting speech and mostly short, simple sentences; suggests inability to use complex sentences and "connectors" when appropriate or required
    - has a markedly nonnative pronunciation, with many phonological errors and/or error patterns, and is sometimes incomprehensible

1
- Is generally incomprehensible, even to a sympathetic listener, despite the listener's constant effort to interpret the intended meaning
- Gives an incomplete and/or mostly inaccurate and/or irrelevant response
- Produces errors and/or error patterns that very often interfere with communication
    - has very little grammatical control (many serious errors and/or error patterns in virtually all structures)
    - employs very little vocabulary, with some "formulaic speech" (memorized phrases, fixed expressions) used inappropriately
    - has virtually no fluency: speech is fragmentary and halting, interrupted often by long pauses and repetitions, and consists only of isolated words, memorized phrases, and fixed expressions
    - has a markedly nonnative pronunciation, with many serious phonological errors and/or error patterns, and is very often incomprehensible

0
- Is completely incomprehensible, even to a sympathetic listener, despite the listener's constant effort to interpret the intended meaning
- Gives an entirely inaccurate/irrelevant response or fails to respond at all
- Produces errors and/or error patterns that always interfere with communication
    - has no grammatical control (many serious errors and/or error patterns in all structures)
    - employs no vocabulary, not even "formulaic speech" (memorized phrases and fixed expressions)
    - has no fluency
    - has a markedly nonnative pronunciation and is always incomprehensible

---

[2] "Sympathetic listener" refers to a native speaker of the language who is accustomed to dealing with nonnative learners of the language. A sympathetic listener tends to make a conscious effort to understand the test taker, interpreting his or her speech for its intended meaning.

Presentational Writing Section

This scoring guide is used to evaluate responses in the Presentational Writing section. The score range is 0 to 4.

4
- Is completely and easily comprehensible, even to an unsympathetic reader[3]
- Gives a complete and entirely accurate, relevant response, with appropriate elaboration, to all (or almost all) parts of the question
- May make sporadic errors, but they rarely or never interfere with communication
    - has strong grammatical control (no errors in basic, high-frequency structures; few errors in complex, low-frequency structures; no marked error patterns)
    - employs a broad, precise vocabulary adequate for almost all topics, with word choice that is generally idiomatic and varied and rarely awkward
    - has very few or no errors in mechanics, which rarely or never interfere with meaning
    - is completely coherent and well organized, with frequent use of complex sentences and "connectors" when appropriate or required
    - uses language that is appropriate for the intended task and/or audience

3
- Is generally comprehensible, even to an unsympathetic reader, but occasionally requires the reader's effort and interpretation of the intended meaning
- Gives a mostly accurate, relevant response to most parts of the question
- Is likely to produce errors and/or error patterns, but they only occasionally interfere with communication
    - has moderate grammatical control (few errors in basic, high-frequency structures; some errors and/or error patterns in complex, low-frequency structures)
    - employs a vocabulary adequate for most general topics, with word choice that is often idiomatic but occasionally awkward
    - makes some errors in mechanics (spelling, punctuation, etc.), but they only occasionally interfere with meaning
    - is generally coherent and organized, with some complex sentences and "connectors" when appropriate or required
    - is likely to use language that is appropriate for the intended task and/or audience

---

[3] "Unsympathetic reader" refers to a native speaker of the language who is NOT accustomed to dealing with nonnative learners of the language. An unsympathetic reader does not make any special effort to understand the test taker.

2
- Is somewhat comprehensible to a sympathetic reader,[4] but often requires the reader's effort and interpretation of the intended meaning
- Gives a somewhat accurate, relevant response to some parts of the question
- Produces errors and/or error patterns that may often interfere with communication
  - has limited grammatical control (many errors and/or error patterns in basic, high-frequency structures; no control of complex, low-frequency structures)
  - employs a limited vocabulary, with word choice that is often unidiomatic and awkward
  - makes several errors in mechanics (spelling, punctuation, etc.), which may often interfere with meaning
  - is partly or often incoherent, with little evidence of organization; suggests inability to use complex sentences and "connectors" when appropriate or required
  - is likely to use language that is inappropriate for the intended task and/or audience

1
- Is generally incomprehensible, even to a sympathetic reader, despite the reader's constant effort to interpret the intended meaning
- Gives an incomplete, mostly inaccurate and/or irrelevant response
- Produces errors and/or error patterns that very often interfere with communication
  - has very little grammatical control (many serious errors and/or error patterns in virtually all structures)
  - employs very little vocabulary, with some "formulaic language" (memorized phrases, fixed expressions) used inappropriately
  - makes many serious errors in mechanics (spelling, punctuation, etc.) in virtually all structures, which very often interfere with meaning
  - is mostly incoherent, with very little or no evidence of organization
  - uses language that is inappropriate for the intended task and/or audience

0
- Is completely incomprehensible, even to a sympathetic reader, despite the reader's constant effort to interpret the intended meaning
- Gives an entirely inaccurate, irrelevant response or fails to respond at all
- Produces errors and/or error patterns that always interfere with communication
  - has no grammatical control (many serious errors and/or error patterns in all structures)
  - employs no vocabulary, not even "formulaic language" (memorized phrases and fixed expressions)
  - makes many serious errors in mechanics (spelling, punctuation, etc.) in all structures, which always interfere with meaning
  - is completely incoherent

---

[4] "Sympathetic reader" refers to a native speaker of the language who is accustomed to dealing with nonnative learners of the language. A sympathetic reader tends to make a conscious effort to understand the test taker, interpreting his or her writing for its intended meaning.

What You Should Know About How the *Spanish: Productive Language Skills* Test Is Scored

As you build your skills in answering constructed-response questions, it is important to have in mind the process used to score the test. If you understand the process by which experts determine your scores, you may have a better context in which to think about your strategies for success.

How the Test Is Scored

After each test administration, test books and recordings are returned to ETS. The test books in which constructed-response answers are written and the recordings that contain the spoken responses are sent to the location of the scoring session.

The scoring sessions usually take place over two days. The sessions are led by scoring leaders, highly qualified Spanish teachers who have many years of experience scoring test questions. All of the remaining scorers are experienced Spanish teachers and Spanish teacher-educators. An effort is made to balance experienced scorers with newer scorers at each session; the experienced scorers provide continuity with past sessions, and the new scorers ensure that new ideas and perspectives are considered and that the pool of scorers remains large enough to cover the test's needs throughout the year.

Preparing to Train the Scorers

The scoring leaders meet several days before the scoring session to assemble the materials for the training portions of the main session. Training scorers is a rigorous process, and it is designed to ensure that each response gets a score that is consistent both with the scores given to other responses and with the overall scoring philosophy and criteria established for the test when it was designed. The scoring leaders review the "General Scoring Guides," which contain the overall criteria for awarding the appropriate score.

To begin identifying appropriate training materials for an individual question, the scoring leaders first listen to and read through many responses to get a sense of the range of answers. They then choose a set of benchmarks, one response at each score level. These benchmarks serve as solid representative examples of the kind of response that meets the scoring criteria at each score level and are considered the foundation for score standards throughout the session.

The scoring leaders then choose a larger set of test-takers' responses to serve as sample responses. These sample responses represent the wide variety of possible responses the scorers might see. The sample responses serve as the basis for practice scoring at the scoring session, so the scorers can rehearse how they will apply the scoring criteria before they begin. The process of choosing a set of benchmark responses and a set of sample responses is followed systematically for each question to be scored at the session.

Training at the Main Scoring Session

At the scoring session, the scorers are placed into groups according to the questions they are assigned to score. New scorers are distributed equally across all groups. One of the scoring leaders is placed with each group. The "chief scorer" is the person who has overall authority over the scoring session and plays a variety of key roles in training and in ensuring consistent and fair scores.

For each question, the training session proceeds in the same way:

1. All scorers carefully listen to or read through the question they will be scoring.

2. All scorers review the "General Scoring Guides."

3. For each question, the leader guides the scorers through the set of benchmark responses, explaining in detail why each response received the score it did. Scorers are encouraged to ask questions and share their perspectives.

4. Scorers then practice on the set of sample responses chosen by the leader. The leader polls the scorers on what scores they would award and then leads a discussion to ensure that there is consensus about the scoring criteria and how they are to be applied.

5. When the leader is confident that the scorers will apply the criteria consistently and accurately, the actual scoring begins.

Quality-Control Processes

A number of procedures are followed to ensure that accuracy of scoring is maintained during the scoring session. Most importantly, each response is scored twice, with the first scorer's decision hidden from the second scorer. If the two scores for a response are the same or differ by only one point, the scoring for that response is considered complete, and the test taker will be awarded the sum of the two scores. If the two scores differ by more than one point, the response is scored by a scoring leader, who has not seen the decisions made by the other two scorers. If this third score is midway between the first two scores, the test taker's score for the question is the sum of the first two scores; otherwise, it is the sum of the third score and whichever of the first two scores is closer to it.

Another way of maintaining scoring accuracy is through back-reading. Throughout the session, the leader for each question checks random samples of scores awarded by all the scorers. If the leader finds that a scorer is not applying the scoring criteria appropriately, that scorer is given more training.

At the beginning of the second day of scoring, additional sets of responses are scored using the consensus method described above. This helps ensure that the scorers are refreshed on the scoring criteria and are applying them consistently.

Finally, the scoring session is designed so that several different scorers (usually four) contribute to any single test taker's total score. This minimizes the effects of a scorer who might score slightly more stringently or generously than other scorers.

The entire scoring process—general scoring guides, standardized benchmarks and samples, consensus scoring, adjudication procedures, back-reading, and rotation of test questions to a variety of scorers—is applied consistently and systematically at every scoring session to ensure comparable scores for each administration and across all administrations of the test.

Given the information above about how constructed responses are scored and what the scorers are looking for in successful responses, you are now ready to look at specific questions, suggestions of how to approach the questions, and sample responses and scores given to those responses.

Chapter 9
Practice Questions—*Spanish: Productive Language Skills*

▶   ▶   ▶   ▶   ▶   ▶   ▶   ▶   ▶   ▶   ▶   ▶

Now that you have worked through preparation and strategies for taking the *Spanish: Productive Language Skills* test, you should take the following practice test. The test questions have appeared on actual Praxis tests, now retired. You will probably find it helpful to simulate actual testing conditions, giving yourself 60 minutes to work on the questions. You can use the lined answer pages provided if you wish.

When you have finished the practice questions, you can read through the sample responses with scorer annotations in chapter 10.

The speaking and listening sections for this practice test are found on the *Spanish* CD included with this study guide. Tracks 6–13 refer to the *Spanish: Productive Language Skills* test. (Note that tracks 1–5 refer to the *Spanish: Content Knowledge* test; you will not need to listen to that section of the CD unless you are planning to take that test as well.)

To simulate actual testing conditions, you might find it helpful to use your own tape recorder to record your responses to the questions presented on this CD. As you listen to the CD, you will notice that pauses have been included in the narration. During the pauses, you may prepare your responses and record your responses on your tape recorder.

As in actual testing conditions, you should not stop your CD player during the practice test.

Keep in mind that the test you take at an actual administration will have different questions. You should not expect your level of performance to be exactly the same as when you take the test at an actual administration, because numerous factors affect a person's performance in any given testing situation.

THE PRAXIS
S E R I E S
Professional Assessments for Beginning Teachers®

TEST NAME:

Spanish: Productive Language Skills (0192)
Practice Questions

Time—60 Minutes

9 Questions

(Note: For questions 1 through 6, you must answer the questions in the time allotted on the CD. For questions 7–9, you will be allotted 35 minutes to answer the questions. If you finish before time is called, you may go back and review your responses to questions 7–9 <u>only</u>.)

PRESENTATIONAL SPEAKING SECTION: Questions 1–6

Time—25 minutes

GENERAL DIRECTIONS

These questions are designed to elicit responses that demonstrate how well you speak Spanish. There are six different questions, and special directions will be given for each one. You will be told how long you have for answering the questions. Although you need not speak for the entire time period, you should give as complete an answer as possible within the time allotted.

As you speak, your voice will be recorded. Your score for these questions will be based only on what is on the recording. Be sure to speak loudly enough for the recording device to record clearly what you say. You are not expected to know all the words you may feel you need. If you do not know specific vocabulary, try to express yourself as well as you can, using circumlocution if necessary. You may take notes in your test book.

Your speaking will be evaluated on the following:

- Overall comprehensibility to a native speaker of Spanish who is not accustomed to dealing with nonnative speakers

- Accuracy and appropriateness of the content

- Presentation of ideas in a related and logical manner, supported by relevant reasons, examples, and details

- Appropriateness of vocabulary

- Accuracy of grammar and pronunciation

- Fluency of delivery and cohesiveness (including use of varied sentence structure and transitional expressions where appropriate)

- Appropriateness for a given task and/or listener

- The extent to which all of the assigned tasks are completed

If you make a mistake and correct it soon afterward, it will not be considered a mistake.

Speaking Section Directions

[The following directions will be heard on the recording.]

This is the Presentational Speaking section of the *Spanish: Productive Language Skills* practice test.

The practice test questions contained on this CD are similar to the kinds of questions you will encounter during an actual test. The test questions you will hear are also printed in the "Practice Questions" chapter of the study guide.

To simulate actual testing conditions, you might find it helpful to use your own tape recorder to record your responses to the questions presented on this CD. As you listen to the CD, you will notice that pauses have been included in the narration. During the pauses, you may prepare your responses and record your responses on your tape recorder.

To simulate actual testing conditions, do not stop your CD player or your tape recorder during the practice test.

In a moment, you will hear an introductory statement by the person who recorded the Spanish portions of Questions One through Six. The purpose of this introduction is to familiarize you with the speaker's voice. Listen to the following passage.

Los alumnos tienen clases de lunes a viernes, excepto los días feriados. Este año, todos los alumnos saldrán temprano de la escuela el 20 y 27 de enero debido a que habrá conferencias para los profesores del colegio.

For each speaking question in the test, you will be given time to prepare your response and time to record your response.

Listen for the voice on the CD to direct you to answer the question; begin speaking only after you have been told to start your response. You will not be given credit for anything recorded during the preparation time.

GO ON TO THE NEXT PAGE

Practice Questions

In this part of the test, you are asked to answer in Spanish two warm-up questions that will not be scored. Listen to the directions for each question.

Practice Question A

Directions: Answer the following question in Spanish. You will have <u>20 seconds</u> to prepare your response. Then you will have <u>20 seconds</u> to record your response. Remember, do not begin speaking until you hear the words "Answer Practice Question A now."

Describa lo que usted hace durante un fin de semana típico.

Practice Question B

Directions: Read aloud the following passage in Spanish. Before you are asked to speak, you will have <u>1 minute</u> to read the passage silently. Then you will have <u>1 minute</u> to record your reading of the passage.

Marta acercó el cajón de las patatas y puso unas cuantas entre la ceniza.

—Vamos a asar patatas y a comerlas cuando estén a punto—dijo. ¡Cosa más rica! . . .

Las patatas iban poniéndose grises y llenas de cenizas y negras por algún lado. Marta las sacaba entonces, soplándose los dedos y todos nos reíamos, hasta Nin, que no sé cómo se daba cuenta de lo que pasaba. Marta las abría por el medio y salía un humito muy pequeño y un olorcillo buenísimo. A mí, que no me gustaban las patatas, aquellas me parecían muy apetitosas. Marta les echaba sal, y así, a mordiscos, medio quemándonos y pelándolas con los dedos, nos las fuimos comiendo. ¡Si nos hubiera visto Susana! Por la ventana de la cocina ya se veía oscuro y allá arriba, muy lejos, brillaban dos estrellitas.

NOTES

GO ON TO THE NEXT PAGE

Question 1

Directions: In this question, you are asked to persuade someone to help you out of a difficult situation by leaving a message in Spanish on a telephone answering machine.

Pretend that you are Roberto or Roberta Díaz. You have just arrived in Buenos Aires, Argentina, to play the first match of a tennis tournament that will take place tomorrow morning. As you unpack, you realize that you left your tennis shoes at home. The only place nearby that sells the kind of shoe you prefer will close in fifteen minutes. You call the shop and you are connected to the telephone answering machine. Record a message in Spanish in which you

- explain the situation;

- say what kind of tennis shoes you want;

- say that you are on your way; and

- try to persuade someone in the shop to keep it open until you arrive.

You will have <u>2 minutes</u> to review the situation and to prepare your message. Then you will have <u>1 1/2 minutes</u> to record your message.

NOTES

GO ON TO THE NEXT PAGE

Question 2

Directions: In this question, you are asked to describe in Spanish the picture in your test book. Do <u>not</u> assume that the person listening can see the picture. In your description, include all of the following details:

- Where this incident is taking place;

- What has just occurred;

- What is probably going to happen next;

- How this situation could have been avoided; and

- What the man or woman probably would say in this situation.

Before you are asked to speak, you will have <u>2 minutes</u> to study the picture and think about your response. Then you will have <u>2 minutes</u> to give your response.

NOTES

GO ON TO THE NEXT PAGE

Question 3

Directions: In this question, you are asked to tell a <u>continuous</u> story in Spanish, based <u>only</u> on what you see in the pictures in your test book. In your story, tell what happened in <u>each</u> of the six pictures, but do <u>not</u> assume that the person listening can see the pictures.

Before you are asked to speak, you will have <u>1 minute</u> to study the pictures and think about your response. Then you will have <u>2 minutes</u> to tell the story. Start the story with the words *"La semana pasada . . . "*

NOTES

GO ON TO THE NEXT PAGE

Question 4

Directions: In this question, you are asked to give your opinion in Spanish on the following subject:

Should all United States university students study a foreign language?

- State and defend your opinion.

- Use specific examples to support your ideas.

You will have <u>1 minute</u> to prepare your response before you are asked to speak. Then you will have <u>2 minutes</u> to give your response.

NOTES

GO ON TO THE NEXT PAGE

Question 5

Directions: In this question, you are asked to paraphrase in Spanish a passage after you have heard it read twice in Spanish. You may take notes in your test book during the readings.

Before you are asked to speak, you will have <u>1 minute</u> to review any notes you may have taken and to prepare your response. Then you will have <u>1 1/2 minutes</u> to paraphrase the passage in Spanish.

NOTES

GO ON TO THE NEXT PAGE

Question 6

Directions: In this question, you are asked to give a brief talk in Spanish based on the following situation.

Pretend that a group of Argentinean secondary school teachers is attending a conference on exchange programs, being held near your hometown. You host a special dinner for the teachers to propose an exchange program between students from their colegio and your local high school. At the dinner, you give a brief talk in Spanish in which you

- welcome the visiting teachers; and

- explain how you think the Argentinean students would benefit from being exchange students in your town.

Be sure to observe the appropriate degree of formality for such a talk.

You will have <u>2 minutes</u> to prepare your talk. Then you will have <u>1 1/2 minutes</u> to give your talk

---

NOTES

STOP.

THIS IS THE END OF THE PRESENTATIONAL SPEAKING SECTION.

AT THE ACTUAL TEST ADMINISTRATION, YOU MUST NOT TURN THE PAGE UNTIL YOU ARE TOLD TO DO SO.

END OF RECORDING.

PRESENTATIONAL WRITING SECTION: Questions 7–9

Time—35 minutes

GENERAL DIRECTIONS

There are three questions in this section. Be sure to answer each question completely. For each question, there is a <u>suggested</u> time limit so that you can pace yourself as you work.

Write your answers in Spanish as clearly and neatly as possible on the lined pages provided. Your written Spanish should be acceptable to a wide range of educated native speakers.

You may use the area marked "NOTES" to plan and take notes on each question. These notes will not be used in evaluating your response.

Your writing will be evaluated on the following:

- Overall comprehensibility to a native speaker of Spanish who is not accustomed to dealing with the writing of nonnative learners

- Accuracy and appropriateness of content

- Presentation of ideas in a related and logical manner, supported by relevant reasons, examples, and details

- Appropriateness of vocabulary

- Accuracy of grammar and mechanics (including spelling and accent marks)

- Cohesiveness (including use of varied sentence structure and transitional expressions where appropriate)

- Appropriateness for a given task and/or reader

- The extent to which all the assigned tasks are completed

Use only the lined pages provided for your response. Although you need not use all of the space on the lined pages provided, you should give as complete a response as possible.

Question 7

(Suggested time—10 minutes)

Directions: In this question, you are asked to write a <u>continuous</u> story in Spanish, based only on the six pictures below. In your story, tell what happened in <u>each</u> of the six pictures, but do <u>not</u> assume that the reader of the story can see the pictures.

Begin your story with the words *"La semana pasada . . ."*

NOTES

Begin your response here.

_____

_____

_____

_____

_____

_____

_____

_____

_____

_____

_____

_____

_____

_____

_____

_____

_____

_____

_____

_____

_____

_____

Question 8

(Suggested time—15 minutes)

Directions: In this question, you are asked to write a formal letter in Spanish based on the following situation.

Pretend that you are Rosa Sánchez or Pablo Ramírez. While you were on vacation in Ecuador, you bought a beautiful hand-carved wooden plate and arranged for it to be shipped to your home. After you returned home, the plate arrived damaged. Write a letter to the store in Quito explaining the situation and persuading the store to resolve the problem promptly. Include the following information:

- When and where you bought the plate

- A description of the plate

- How you paid for the plate

- What the problem is

- What you want the store to do

Be sure to observe the appropriate degree of formality for such a letter.

NOTES

Begin your response here.

_____

_____

_____

_____

_____

_____

_____

_____

_____

_____

_____

_____

_____

_____

_____

_____

_____

_____

_____

_____

_____

Question 9

(Suggested time—10 minutes)

Directions: In this question, you are asked to write four questions in Spanish based on the following situation:

Pretend that you are writing an article about a dignitary from a Spanish-speaking country—for example, a government official or a famous writer. This person has agreed to help you by answering four questions that you will send to him or her in the mail.

In the lined space provided on the next page, write in complete Spanish sentences the four questions that you wish to ask.

Your questions should include a variety of question types. Ask

- one question that requires only a short answer; and

- three questions that require a longer answer, such as an opinion, a description, a comparison, or a narration.

Be sure to observe the appropriate degree of formality for the purpose of your questionnaire.

NOTES

First Question _____

_____

_____

_____

Second Question _____

_____

_____

_____

Third Question _____

_____

_____

_____

Fourth Question _____

_____

_____

_____

STOP

THIS IS THE END OF THE TEST.

If you finish before time is called, you may go back and review your responses to Questions 7–9 only.

Chapter 10

Sample Responses and How They Were Scored—
Spanish: Productive Language Skills

▶ ▶ ▶ ▶ ▶ ▶ ▶ ▶ ▶ ▶ ▶ ▶

This chapter presents actual sample responses to the practice questions in chapter 9 and explanations for the scores the responses received. After you have finished responding to the practice questions in chapter 9, review your answers in light of the scored sample answers. If you find it difficult to evaluate your answers and assign them scores, ask a colleague, a professor, or a practicing teacher for help.

As discussed in chapter 8, each constructed-response question on the Praxis *Spanish: Productive Language Skills* test is scored on a scale from 0 to 4. The scoring guides used to score these questions are repeated here for your convenience.

General Scoring Guides for the *Spanish: Productive Language Skills* Test

Presentational Speaking Section

This scoring guide is used to evaluate responses in the Presentational Speaking section. The score range is 0 to 4.

4
- Is completely and easily comprehensible, even to an unsympathetic listener[1]

- Gives a complete and entirely accurate, relevant response, with appropriate elaboration, to all (or almost all) parts of the question

- May make sporadic errors, but they rarely or never interfere with communication

  — has strong grammatical control (no errors in basic, high-frequency structures; few errors in complex, low-frequency structures; no marked error patterns)

  — employs a broad, precise vocabulary adequate for almost all topics, with word choice that is generally idiomatic and varied and rarely awkward

  — has overall fluency: speech is occasionally or rarely hesitant, with frequent use of complex sentences and "connectors" when appropriate or required

  — may have a slightly nonnative pronunciation, with few or no phonological errors and no error patterns, but is always comprehensible

3
- Is generally comprehensible, even to an unsympathetic listener, but occasionally requires the listener's effort and interpretation of the intended meaning

- Gives a mostly accurate, relevant response to most parts of the question

- Is likely to make errors and/or produce error patterns, but they only occasionally interfere with communication

  — has moderate grammatical control (few errors in basic, high-frequency structures; some errors and/or error patterns in complex, low-frequency structures)

  — employs vocabulary adequate for most general topics, with word choice that is often idiomatic but occasionally awkward

  — has considerable fluency: speech is sometimes hesitant, with some use of complex sentences and "connectors" when appropriate or required

  — may have a markedly nonnative pronunciation with some phonological errors and/or error patterns, but is nearly or always comprehensible

---

[1] "Unsympathetic listener" refers to a native speaker of the language who is NOT accustomed to dealing with nonnative learners of the language. An unsympathetic listener does not make any special effort to understand the test taker.

2
- Is somewhat comprehensible to a sympathetic listener[2], but often requires the listener's effort and interpretation of the intended meaning

- Gives a somewhat accurate, relevant response to some parts of the question

- Produces errors and/or error patterns that may often interfere with communication
  - has limited grammatical control (many errors and/or error patterns in basic, high-frequency structures; no control of complex, low-frequency structures)
  - employs a limited vocabulary, with word choice that is often unidiomatic and awkward
  - has limited fluency, with halting speech and mostly short, simple sentences; suggests inability to use complex sentences and "connectors" when appropriate or required
  - has a markedly nonnative pronunciation, with many phonological errors and/or error patterns, and is sometimes incomprehensible

1
- Is generally incomprehensible, even to a sympathetic listener, despite the listener's constant effort to interpret the intended meaning

- Gives an incomplete and/or mostly inaccurate and/or irrelevant response

- Produces errors and/or error patterns that very often interfere with communication
  - has very little grammatical control (many serious errors and/or error patterns in virtually all structures)
  - employs very little vocabulary, with some "formulaic speech" (memorized phrases, fixed expressions) used inappropriately
  - has virtually no fluency: speech is fragmentary and halting, interrupted often by long pauses and repetitions, and consists only of isolated words, memorized phrases, and fixed expressions
  - has a markedly nonnative pronunciation, with many serious phonological errors and/or error patterns, and is very often incomprehensible

0
- Is completely incomprehensible, even to a sympathetic listener, despite the listener's constant effort to interpret the intended meaning

- Gives an entirely inaccurate, irrelevant response or fails to respond at all

- Produces errors and/or error patterns that always interfere with communication
  - has no grammatical control (many serious errors and/or error patterns in all structures)
  - employs no vocabulary, not even "formulaic speech" (memorized phrases and fixed expressions)
  - has no fluency
  - has a markedly nonnative pronunciation and is always incomprehensible

---

[2] "Sympathetic listener" refers to a native speaker of the language who is accustomed to dealing with nonnative learners of the language. A sympathetic listener tends to make a conscious effort to understand the test taker, interpreting his or her speech for its intended meaning.

Presentational Writing Section

This scoring guide is used to evaluate reponses in the Presentational Writing Section. The score range is 0 to 4.

4
- Is completely and easily comprehensible, even to an unsympathetic reader[3]

- Gives a complete and entirely accurate, relevant response, with appropriate elaboration, to all (or almost all) parts of the question

- May make sporadic errors, but they rarely or never interfere with communication

    — has strong grammatical control (no errors in basic, high-frequency structures; few errors in complex, low-frequency structures; no marked error patterns)

    — employs a broad, precise vocabulary adequate for almost all topics, with word choice that is generally idiomatic and varied and rarely awkward

    — has very few or no errors in mechanics, which rarely or never interfere with meaning

    — is completely coherent and well organized, with frequent use of complex sentences and "connectors" when appropriate or required

    — uses language that is appropriate for the intended task and/or audience

3
- Is generally comprehensible, even to an unsympathetic reader, but occasionally requires the reader's effort and interpretation of the intended meaning

- Gives a mostly accurate, relevant response to most parts of the question

- Is likely to produce errors and/or error patterns, but they only occasionally interfere with communication

    — has moderate grammatical control (few errors in basic, high-frequency structures; some errors and/or error patterns in complex, low-frequency structures)

    — employs a vocabulary adequate for most general topics, with word choice that is often idiomatic but occasionally awkward

    — makes some errors in mechanics (spelling, punctuation, etc.), but they only occasionally interfere with meaning

    — is generally coherent and organized, with some complex sentences and "connectors" when appropriate or required

    — is likely to use language that is appropriate for the intended task and/or audience

---

[3] "Unsympathetic reader" refers to a native speaker of the language who is NOT accustomed to dealing with nonnative learners of the language. An unsympathetic reader does not make any special effort to understand the test taker.

2 ■ Is somewhat comprehensible to a sympathetic reader,[4] but often requires the reader's effort and interpretation of the intended meaning

■ Gives a somewhat accurate, relevant response to some parts of the question

■ Produces errors and/or error patterns that may often interfere with communication

— has limited grammatical control (many errors and/or error patterns in basic, high-frequency structures; no control of complex, low-frequency structures)

— employs a limited vocabulary, with word choice that is often unidiomatic and awkward

— makes several errors in mechanics (spelling, punctuation, etc.), which may often interfere with meaning

— is partly or often incoherent, with little evidence of organization; suggests inability to use complex sentences and "connectors" when appropriate or required

— is likely to use language that is inappropriate for the intended task and/or audience

1 ■ Is generally incomprehensible, even to a sympathetic reader, despite the reader's constant effort to interpret the intended meaning

■ Gives an incomplete, mostly inaccurate and/or irrelevant response

■ Produces errors and/or error patterns that very often interfere with communication

— has very little grammatical control (many serious errors and/or error patterns in virtually all structures)

— employs very little vocabulary, with some "formulaic language" (memorized phrases, fixed expressions) used inappropriately

— makes many serious errors in mechanics (spelling, punctuation, etc.) in virtually all structures, which very often interfere with meaning

— is mostly incoherent, with very little or no evidence of organization

— uses language that is inappropriate for the intended task and/or audience

0 ■ Is completely incomprehensible, even to a sympathetic reader, despite the reader's constant effort to interpret the intended meaning

■ Gives an entirely inaccurate, irrelevant response or fails to respond at all

■ Produces errors and/or error patterns that always interfere with communication

— has no grammatical control (many serious errors and/or error patterns in all structures)

— employs no vocabulary, not even "formulaic language" (memorized phrases and fixed expressions)

— makes many serious errors in mechanics (spelling, punctuation, etc.) in all structures, which always interfere with meaning

— is completely incoherent

---

[4] "Sympathetic reader" refers to a native speaker of the language who is accustomed to dealing with nonnative learners of the language. A sympathetic reader tends to make a conscious effort to understand the test taker, interpreting his or her writing for its intended meaning.

Presentational Speaking Section

Constructed-Response Question 1—Sample Responses

We will now look at four scored responses to the first constructed-response practice question ("Tennis Player Leaves Phone Message") and see comments from the scoring leader about why each response received the score it did.

Sample Response 1: Score of 4

> Buenas tardes, me llamo Roberto Díaz. Soy el famoso jugador de tenis. A lo mejor Uds. me han visto en la tele . . . . Y estoy aquí en Buenos Aires para participar en el torte, torneo de tenis que va a empezar mañana, y yo voy a jugar en el primer partido mañana, y es que estoy en una situación muy difícil, y lo que pas, lo que pasa es que acabo de darme cuenta de que se me olvidaron mis zapatos de tenis allí en Madrid, y es una situación muy vergonzosa pero les ruego que Uds. me ayuden. Ahh, yo sé que Uds. van a cerrar en quince minutos, y, pues, mi hotel está muy cerca a, a su tienda, y les pido que alguien . . . del personal allí de su tienda se quede allí y me espere. Ahorita estoy en camino a . . . a su tienda. Estoy hablando con mi teléfono celular y voy a llegar, yo creo, muy pronto. Si Uds. pudieran, ahh, apartar para mí unos zapatos "Niqe Fast Jackson," ahh, del color morado—ese es mi favorito—pues, les agradecería mucho. Por favor, necesito su ayuda . . . ahh . . . y espero que me puedan ayudar.

Commentary on Sample Response That Earned a Score of 4

This oral response clearly demonstrates proficiency. The test taker has successfully completed the task of leaving a persuasive message on a telephone answering machine. The sample includes all of the requested information, which is accurate and relevant, with appropriate elaboration. After stating his name, the test taker adds: *Soy el famoso jugador de tenis. A lo mejor Uds. me han visto en la tele.* There is strong grammatical control, with accurate, idiomatic, precise vocabulary: *lo que pasa es que acabo de darme cuenta de que se me olvidaron mis zapatos de tenis allí en Madrid.* The expressions *darse cuenta de, acabar de,* and the reflexive *olvidarse* reflect control of idiomatic language. There is use of complex sentences and the subjunctive tense: *les pido que alguien . . . del personal allí de su tienda se quede allí y me espere* (present indicative and present subjunctive); and *Si Uds. pudieran . . . apartar para mí unos zapatos . . . pues, les agradecería mucho* (imperfect subjunctive and conditional). There is overall fluency, with occasional hesitancy in speech and some self-correction: *para participar en el torte, torneo.* The oral response has a natural flow, is completely and easily comprehensible, and merits a score of 4.

Sample Response 2: Score of 3

> Buenas tardes. Por favor, acabo de llegar en Buenos Aires para jugar tenis en un campioneta mañana por la mañana, muy temprano mañana. Y no sé cómo, pero se me olvidaron mis zapatos de tenis, y claro, que no puedo com, jugar mañana sin mis zapatos. Por favor, podría qued, quedarse alguien en la zapatería para que yo pueda comprar unos zapatos de tenis "Niqe." Me voy ahora mismo, y puedo llegar muy pronto. Por favor, espéreme . . . para que puedo comprar los zapatos que necesito tanto. Muchísimas gracias.

Commentary on Sample Response That Earned a Score of 3

This oral sample is generally comprehensible, but occasionally requires the listener's effort. The response includes most of the assigned tasks but without elaboration. The content is relevant, but the sample is rather brief. The test taker does not identify himself as is anticipated in the prompt, nor does he clarify the urgency of the situation. There is moderate grammatical control, with a few errors in basic structures and vocabulary: *acabo de llegar en (a) Buenos Aires para jugar (al) tenis en un campioneta (campeonato).* The word choice is adequate and often idiomatic: *acabo de llegar, se me olvidaron mis zapatos de tenis, me voy ahora mismo.* There is also some alliterative repetition: *mañana por la mañana, muy temprano mañana.* There is control of the verb forms, as in the use of subjunctive with *para que*: *Por favor, podría qued, quedarse alguien . . . para que yo pueda comprar,* but there are also occasional lapses, such as *espéreme . . . para que puedo (pueda) comprar los zapatos* (imperative with present indicative [subjunctive]). The test taker demonstrates considerable fluency, with good pronunciation. There is a flow to the sample that suggests proficiency and merits a score of 3.

Sample Response 3: Score of 2

> Hola. Yo soy Roberto Díaz de los Estados Unidos y en la mañana tengo un partito de tenis. Me olvide mis zapatos de tenis en mi país y es muy importante que tenga algunas para, algunas pare . . . para mi partita en la mañana. Quiero "Atlidas" para las mujeres, tomaño nueve. Estoy saliendo ahora para venir a su tienda. Por favor, es un emergencia. Si pueda, será abierto cuando llegue. Mil gracias si puede hacer este, para mí . . . Muchísimo gracias.

Commentary on Sample Response That Earned a Score of 2

The sample is somewhat comprehensible but often requires the listener's effort to interpret the intended meaning. The information is relevant and somewhat accurate, but errors interfere with communication: *Me olvide (olvidé).* The omission of the accent to indicate the preterite tense changes the meaning—the past is the intended tense in this sentence. In *Estoy saliendo ahora para venir (ir) a su tienda,* the customer is leaving in order to go, not come, to the store. The word choice is unidiomatic: *en (por) la mañana;* incorrect: *un partito (partido) de tenis; para mi partita (partido); tomaño (tamaño) nueve;* or lacks agreement: *algunas (algunos),* referring to *zapatos; un (una) emergencia; Muchísimo (Muchísimas) gracias.* There is some successful use of the subjunctive tense: *es muy importante que tenga;* even when it frames an awkward, incorrect phrase: *Si pueda, será abierto cuando llegue,* which implores the store owner to stay open if possible until he arrives. This twisted sentence indicates language interference and an inability to use complex sentences. The response lacks overall completeness in that the situation is not adequately explained. The brief, condensed response suggests a lack of proficiency in completing the assigned task. It therefore receives a score of 2.

Sample Response 4: Score of 1

> Hola. Me llamo Rober, Roberta Díaz. No tengo zapatos de tenis por . . . por la
> . . . equipo de tenis. Yo los dejé míos a la casa. Necesito zapatas, pero no llegaré
> a la za, zapatería antes de que est, estaré cerrada. Umm. ¿Puedo esperarme?

Commentary on Sample Response That Earned a Score of 1

This response demonstrates a lack of proficiency in completing the assigned task of communicating a message on a telephone answering machine. A sympathetic listener may understand some elements of the situation, but very often errors interfere with communication. The sample is incomplete, with limited grammatical control. While the opening informal greeting and first sentence are correct: *Hola. Me llamo Rober, Roberta Díaz,* the following sentences all contain errors: *No tengo zapatos de tenis por . . . por (para) la (el) . . . equipo (partido o torneo) de tenis. Yo los dejé míos (los míos) a la casa (en casa). Necesito zapatas (zapatos) . . . antes de que est, estaré (esté) cerrada. ¿Puedo (Puede Ud.) esperarme?* While there are a number of correct verb forms at the beginning of the sample, there is a breakdown at the end, which leaves the listener confused and indicates a lack of fluency. The test taker has very few vocabulary resources to communicate the task. This response merits a score of only 1.

Constructed-Response Question 2—Sample Responses

We will now look at four scored responses to the second constructed-response practice question ("Rain in the City") and see comments from the scoring leader about why each response received the score it did.

Sample Response 1: Score of 4

> En este dibujo hay un hombre y una, una mujer, una pareja, y parece que están
> saliendo de la oficina después de un día de trabajo. Él tiene su traje, y su
> portafolios, y la mujer está vestida muy bien, y iban caminando muy cerca de la
> calle en la acera y pasa un coche y les echa agua sucio al, al hombre y a la mujer,
> también, y creo que lo que va a pasar es que ellos van a tener que encontrar una
> manera de limpiarse porque el lodo y el agua sucia va a manchar su ropa, y creo
> que si ellos, como está lloviendo en el dibujo, si ellos hubieran pensado mejor de
> que estaba lloviendo y si no hubieran estado caminando tan cerca de la calle,
> pero más cerca de la oficina, que el conductor del coche no les hubiera
> manchado con el agua sucio. Y creo que, el hombre o, o, la mujer que dirían en
> esta situación, que estaban muy enojados. Entonces, creo que gritarían al
> conductor del coche, y que le dirían a él que él era muy estúpido por mancharles
> con el agua y por ensuciarles y que la mujer y el hombre echarían la culpa al
> conductor y no a ellos mismos que el conductor tenía, tenía el culpe, la culpa, y

> no ellos. Creo que ellos necesitan pensar mejor si ven que está lloviendo y que hay agua en la calle, que necesitan tener mucho más cuidado para no caminar tan cerca para evadir otra situación así.

Commentary on Sample Response That Earned a Score of 4

In this picture description, the response is completely comprehensible and rarely requires the listener's effort to understand the intended meaning. The test taker responds to all of the five questions in the prompt with strong grammatical control, few errors, and appropriate elaboration: (1) Where the incident is taking place: *parece que están saliendo de la oficina después de un día de trabajo . . . iban caminando muy cerca de la calle en la acera*; (2) What has just occurred: *pasa un coche y les echa agua sucio (sucia)* (stated in the narrative present, though it could have been done in the past tense); (3) What is going to happen next: *creo que lo que va a pasar es que ellos van a tener que encontrar una manera de limpiarse porque el lodo y el agua sucia va (van) a manchar su ropa;* (4) What the man or woman probably would say in this situation: *dirían . . . que estaban muy enojados. Entonces, creo que gritarían al conductor del coche . . . que el conductor tenía . . . la culpa y no ellos;* (5) How the situation could have been avoided, *si ellos hubieran pensado mejor de que estaba lloviendo y si no hubieran estado caminando tan cerca de la calle . . . , el conductor del coche no les hubiera manchado con el agua sucio (sucia).* (Note the use of complex structures.) There is self-correction: *el culpe – la culpa* and an agreement error: *agua sucio – sucia.* The vocabulary is precise and generally idiomatic. The sample ends with a good concluding statement: *Creo que ellos necesitan pensar mejor si ven que está lloviendo y que hay agua en la calle, que necesitan tener mucho más cuidado . . . para evadir otra situación así.* The test taker has communicated the task very effectively with overall fluency and good pronunciation. This is a very full speech sample that clearly demonstrates proficiency and merits a score of 4.

Sample Response 2: Score of 3

> Dibujo, en donde se nota un hombre y una mujer, y están en una ciudad. Está lloviendo mucho y están sent, están parados en el banquete, cerca de la calle. El hombre y la mujer tienen un paraguas y hay un carro que pasa, y por las llantas, ha tirado lodo a la mujer y al hombre. Ya se han ensuciadas por el lodo del carro. La cosa es que ellos estaban parados muy cerca de la calle y por eso . . . pasó, por eso el carro tiró todo el lodo a ellos. Si no, amm, paraban así, eso no hu, no lo hubiera pasado. Se van a, a enojar porque están, están sucios, y se nota que tienen ropa de moda. Y, por seguro van a decir, que est, estén enojados . . . . Es que, también se nota que . . . las caras que est, están tan sorprendidos de tanto lodo que ha tirado el carro.

Commentary on Sample Response That Earned a Score of 3

This speech sample is generally comprehensible even to an unsympathetic listener. The response includes most of the tasks, and the content is mostly accurate and relevant. There is moderate grammatical control. What is notable in this sample is a certain awkwardness at the beginning of the presentation: *Dibujo, en donde se nota un hombre y una mujer, y están en una ciudad.* The vocabulary is adequate, often idiomatic, but, regarding the impersonal and reflexive uses, relies too much on repetition: *Se nota un hombre y una mujer, se han ensuciadas (ensuciados), se nota que tienen ropa de moda, también se nota que.* It is possible to visualize the action in the picture because of the details provided: *hay un carro que pasa, y por las llantas, ha tirado lodo a la mujer y al hombre, Ya se han ensuciadas (ensuciados) por el lodo del carro, por eso el carro tiró todo el lodo a ellos, están tan sorprendidos de tanto lodo que ha tirado el carro,* although this overemphasizes the passing car throwing or splashing mud on the couple. There is also repetition of the verb *estar* in the picture sequence: *están en una ciudad, Está lloviendo mucho, están parados en el banquete, ellos estaban parados muy cerca de la calle, están sucios, estén (están) enojados, están tan sorprendidos.* There is fluency in the response, though speech is sometimes hesitant. The pronunciation is good and the overall sample, which suggests proficiency, merits a score of 3.

Sample Response 3: Score of 2

Esto situación están en un calle. No es un buen día. Lleve a cántaros y hay dos personas que están esperando para un camión o un combi y las dos tienen paraguas y las dos también . . . están de moda y, mmm, tie, tienen ropa muy elegante, pero, es, está lloviendo y porque de la lluvia . . . tienen paraguas. Próximo, aah, también, hay un coche . . . en la calle, y la coche está muy cerca de las dos personas que están a la derecha. Y porque de la lluvia . . . las, probablemente, las dos . . . personas van a tener mucho agua sobre sus cuerpos desde el coche. Y próximo, las personas probablemente van a estar un poco enojados y van a decir algo a la persona que está manejando el coche. Esta situación no es ovidable, porque . . . mmhm, siempre hay lluvia especialmente en el noroeste del país. Y, las dos personas, mmm, si es posible, ellos pueden . . . caminar a otro lugar en la calle, pero, en realidad esta situación ocurrió cada día, especialmente en el otoño y el invierno. Probablemente, ellos.

Commentary on Sample Response That Earned a Score of 2

The oral response is somewhat comprehensible, but often the listener must make an effort to understand the intended meaning. The test taker makes an effort to address the assigned tasks, but the content lacks accuracy and relevancy. The limited grammatical control is evident in the first sentence: *Esto (Esta) situación están (está u ocurre) en un (una) calle.* There is a lack of agreement: *mucho (mucha) agua;* and errors in idiomatic usage: *están esperando para (esperando) un camión.* The vocabulary is limited, with much attention given to the weather: *Lleve (Llueve) a cántaros; las (los) dos tienen paraguas; porque (a causa) de la lluvia; siempre hay lluvia especialmente en el noroeste del país.* There is limited fluency, marked by awkwardness and hesitation in the delivery. The error patterns often interfere with communication, and, therefore, this response suggests a lack of proficiency and earns a score of 2.

Sample Response 4: Score of 1

Dos pera, dos personas está en un calle afuera de, uhh, afuera de la, las casas. Un carro les pasó, les pasan. Un carro les pasan y está tirando agua en ellos. Las personas las pona, las personas van a ser, van a ser enojados en un momento porque sus r –, su ropa, van a, uhh, . . . van a ser muy sucio. Ahh, si ellos, uhh, hubieran movido atrás, un poquito más atrás, no habrían enojados durante esta tiempo porque la agua no va a . . . el agua no va a, a mojarse, a mojarseles. El hombre, probablemente, el hombre, ahh, hubiera gritando, "¡Oye! ¡Niños! ¿Qué está pasando ahorita? ¡Por favor!" Y, también, ahh, va a, hubiera decido, hubiera decido, "Fíjate, señora. ¡El agua!"

Commentary on Sample Response That Earned a Score of 1

This sample is generally incomprehensible despite the listener's constant effort to interpret the intended meaning. The response attempts to describe the picture, but the errors often interfere with communication. There is very little grammatical control, with errors in virtually all structures: *Dos pera, personas está (están) en un (una) calle afuera de, uhh, afuera de la, las casas.* The lack of control of verbs is evident: *si ellos, uhh, hubieran movido atrás; el hombre, ahh, hubiera (habría) gritando (gritado); hubiera (habría) decido (dicho).* There is virtually no fluency. Speech is halting and interrupted by pauses and repetitions. There are attempts at self-correction, not always successful: *Dos pera, dos personas; Un carro les pasó, les pasan (pasa). Un carro les pasan (pasa).* The content does not make much sense: *Las personas las pona, las personas van a ser, van a ser enojados en un momento porque sus r-, su ropa, van a, uhh, . . . van a ser muy sucio.* It is difficult for the listener to follow the description without seeing the picture. The response is a demonstration of a lack of proficiency and receives a score of 1.

Constructed-Response Question 3—Sample Responses

We will now look at four scored responses to the third constructed-response practice question ("New Glasses") and see comments from the scoring leader about why each response received the score it did.

Sample Response 1: Score of 4

Mi padre es, estaba llegando a la casa con una carga pesada de cajas de libros en sus manos. Subiendo la escalera, se resbaló con el periódico que estaba en las escalinatas y, al resbalarse, se le cayeron sus lentes, y se rompieron. Mi madre estaba sentada en el balcón. Se levantó a ayudarle. Ahh, recogió las cajas y mi padre pudo conseguir sus lentes. Ehh, cuan, como vio que estaban rotos, se fue hasta la óptica a tratar de que se los arreglaran. Cuando llegó a la óptica, amm, la señora que trabaja en la óptica le ayudó muy amablemente, amm, a arreglar sus lentes . . . arreglar sus lentes. Y, umm, mi padre pudo salir con sus lentes, mmm, de la óptica, totalmente arreglados . . . . Los lentes, perdón, los lentes no se rompieron, los lentes simplemente se doblaron al caerse y cuando se golpearon con las escalinatas. Por lo tanto, ese mismo día, cuando fue a la óptica la señora de la óptica se les pudo, a, le pudo arreglar los, los, marcos del lente, que estaban dañados, y mi padre pudo salir con sus lentes de la óptica como si estuvieran nuevos.

Commentary on Sample Response That Earned a Score of 4

This oral response is completely comprehensible even to an unsympathetic listener and rarely requires the listener's effort to interpret the intended meaning. The test taker has included all of the assigned tasks with appropriate elaboration in his account of the action in the six-picture sequence. He has set the scene with the past progressive: *Mi padre es, estaba llegando a la casa;* the present participle: *Subiendo la escalera;* and the past participle used as an adjective: *Mi madre estaba sentada.* There is a shift to the preterite for completed actions in the past. There is good use of reflexive forms throughout the description: *se resbaló; al resbalarse, se le cayeron sus lentes y se rompieron; se levantó; se fue; se los arreglaran; no se rompieron; se doblaron al caerse y cuando se golpearon con las escalinatas.* The content is relevant, but the test taker does change his mind as to whether the lenses of the glasses are broken or the frames just needed adjusting: *perdón, los lentes no se rompieron, los lentes simplemente se doblaron al caerse y cuando se golpearon con las escalinatas.* He then explains: *la señora de la óptica . . . le pudo arreglar los, los, marcos del lente (de los lentes), que estaban dañados.* There is use of the subjunctive: *se fue hasta la óptica a tratar de que se los arreglaran;* and the use of the phrase *como si: mi padre pudo salir con sus lentes de la óptica como si estuvieran nuevos.* There is broad vocabulary, and the word choice is generally idiomatic: *con una carga pesada de cajas de libros en sus (las) manos;* and complex sentences are used: *la señora que trabaja en la óptica le ayudó muy amablemente, amm, a arreglar sus lentes.* Though there is occasional hesitancy, the overall presentation, with good pronunciation, indicates fluency. The speech sample is a demonstration of proficiency and merits a score of 4.

Sample Response 2: Score of 3

La semana pasada, José llegó a casa y Ana estaba sentado en el pórtico. Había un periódico en las escaleras y José tropezó en el periódico. Se cayó, y las cajas en sus manos se cayeron. También, se rompió sus gafas. José fue al, uhh, óptico, umm, y, en el, en el óptico, uhh, sentó, se, se sentó con, umm, una mujer y, a encontrar nuevas gafas. Bueno, sal, salió del óptico con nuevas gafas muy contento y mucho mejor.

Commentary on Sample Response That Earned a Score of 3

The response is suggestive of proficiency. While it is generally comprehensible and may occasionally require the listener's effort to understand the intended meaning, it also lacks elaboration. The sample is a very brief description of the content of the six pictures. Moderate grammatical control, with correct verb usage, especially of the preterite and imperfect tenses, along with adequate vocabulary, characterizes this speech sample: *La semana pasada, José llegó a casa y Ana estaba sentado (sentada) en el pórtico.* The test taker communicates the basic information of the six-picture sequence in six sentences. The overall speech sample, delivered with good pronunciation, nevertheless merits a score of 3.

Sample Response 3: Score of 2

Año pasado, Jorge fue a la casa de María y dar sus documentos a ella. Mientras, caminado arriba los pasos a la casa, Jorge se cayó . . . un el, un, los pasos. Y . . . sus anteojos se rompieron . . . María ayudó Jorge, Jorge, y . . . Jorge fue a la optom . . . itrista, optometrista. Lleva nuevas, nuevos anteojos con, a Jorge. Jorge, Jorge salió la tienda de anteojos alegre.

Commentary on Sample Response That Earned a Score of 2

This oral sample is somewhat comprehensible to a sympathetic listener but often requires the listener's effort to interpret the intended meaning. The brief sample has relevant content but limited grammatical control and vocabulary. The story begins well, then falls apart: *(El) Año (año) pasado, Jorge fue a la casa de María y dar (le dio) sus documentos a ella.* The latter part is not true—he did not give the documents to her. Most of the verbs are in the correct preterite form: *Jorge fue . . . se cayó . . . sus anteojos se rompieron . . . María ayudó (a) Jorge . . . Jorge fue . . . Jorge salió.* There is no use of the imperfect tense for description to contrast with the preterite. There is some use of the present tense also: *Lleva nuevas, nuevos anteojos.* Some word choice is awkward: *Mientras, caminado arriba los pasos a la casa (Subiendo la escalera),* indicating language interference. This sketchy account is told with limited fluency. The speech is halting, told mostly in short sentences, which suggests an inability to use complex structures and connectors. The response indicates a lack of proficiency in completing the oral task and earns a score of 2.

Sample Response 4: Score of 1

Que la semana pasada Carlos está llevando tres cas, cajas cuando ella, umm, regresará . . . mmm . . . cuando ella, él regres, regresó a su casa. Cuando, cuando llegó a su casa, él empezaba a subir las escaleras, pero, desafortun . . . desafortunamente había un periódico que él no veía. Y . . . atrapó. Sus cajas . . . vuelan . . . volían a todos los partes y los papeles también. Su mamá, que estaba sentando se, en, en una silla en, enfrente de la casa, subió para ayudarlo. La, las gafas que tenía Carlos . . . ahora estaba rota. Estuvo, estuvo rota, amm, durante el accidente. Carlos . . . iba a un . . . umm, a una tienda de gafas, umm, para arregle, arreglar sus gafas. La mujer allí, ayud, lo ayudaba y ella . . . hace, hacía las, ahh, las gafas como nuevo.

Commentary on Sample Response That Earned a Score of 1

This oral sample is generally incomprehensible despite the listener's constant effort to interpret the intended meaning. There is some confusion between the use of *ella* and *él,* the test taker oddly not realizing that Carlos is a name for a male: *Que la semana pasada Carlos está llevando tres cas, cajas cuando ella, umm, regresará . . . mmm . . . cuando ella, él regres, regresó a su casa.* The speaker uses the future form, then an unfinished form, before he says the correct preterite form. He then continues his description: *Cuando, cuando . . . él empezaba a subir las escaleras . . . desafortun . . . desafortunamente . . . atrapó.* There is very little vocabulary and little grammatical control. Verb forms are confused: *volían* for *volaban* or *volaron; estaba sentando se* for *estaba sentada.* There is virtually no fluency; the sample is characterized by fragmentary, halting speech, interrupted by long pauses as the test taker struggles to express himself. This response is a demonstration of a lack of proficiency and is given a score of 1.

Constructed-Response Question 4—Sample Responses

We will now look at four scored responses to the fourth constructed-response practice question ("Opinion—Foreign Languages") and see comments from the scoring leader about why each response received the score it did.

Sample Response 1: Score of 4

Yo creo que los estudiantes de la universidad sí deberían estudiar un lenguaje que nos, que ellos no habían aprendido desde chiquitos, desde niños. Esto es muy impor, aprender otro lenguaje es muy importante, porque tiene muchos beneficios para la, el estudiante. Primeramente, podrán hablar con otras personas que no entienden el español o el, el inglés. Pueden comunicarse con, con las personas, umm, que no pueden hablar el idioma que ellos aprendieron desde chiquitos, también adquirirán un entendimiento sobre otras culturas y otras lenguas que ellos no han sido expuestos, desde niños. También, hay más posibilidades de un trabaj, de encontrar un trabajo, si una persona es, umm, multilingual, o, emm, si, si sabe otras, otras lenguas. Umm, también, cuando una persona vaya a otros países . . . de vacaciones, ellos podrán comunicarse con las personas que están en ese país. Así podrán entenderse más, y la persona, el estudiante de la universidad, podrá . . . hablar, y agarrar, obten cosas que no podrá obten, no podría haber obtenido si no hubiese entendido el lenguaje del país que está visitando.

Commentary on Sample Response That Earned a Score of 4

This speech sample regarding the test taker's opinion on whether university students should be required to study a foreign language is comprehensible even to an unsympathetic listener. The content of the response is accurate and relevant: *aprender otro lenguaje es muy importante, porque tiene muchos beneficios para la, el estudiante.* The test taker then proceeds to list and discuss the benefits: *Primeramente, podrán hablar con otras personas que no entienden el español o el, el inglés . . . también adquirirán un entendimiento sobre otras culturas y otras lenguas . . . También, hay más posibilidades de un trabaj, de encontrar un trabajo, si una persona es, umm, multilingual.* There is strong grammatical control and use of a variety of verb tenses, especially the future and conditional, as well as the subjunctive: *cuando una persona vaya a otros países . . . de vacaciones, ellos podrán comunicarse con las personas que están es ese país;* but there is a shift of person, from singular to plural. There is also an incomplete adverbial conjunction: *un entendimiento sobre otras culturas y otras lenguas que (a las que/cuales) ellos no han sido expuestos.* The response concludes with the use of the subjunctive in a complex construction: *Así podrán entenderse más, y la persona, el estudiante de la universidad, podrá . . . hablar, y agarrar, obten cosas que no podrá obten (obtener), no podría haber obtenido si no hubiese entendido el lenguaje del país.* The vocabulary is broad, appropriate, and generally idiomatic for the task. There is occasional hesitancy with overall fluency and good pronunciation. The response demonstrates oral proficiency and merits a score of 4.

Sample Response 2: Score of 3

Creo que no es necesario que todos los estudiantes estadounidenses tienen que estudiar una idioma en la, la universidad. Creo que no es necesario porque, aunque hay muchos beneficios para los estudiantes de una lengua, como un entendimiento de la cultura, como, o un, un entendimiento de otra grupo de gente—todos esos beneficios—ahh, también, hay unos, ahh, desventajas. Por ejemplo, muchos carreras como ingeniería ya tienen muchos cursos, toma mucho tiempo, y sería muy difícil para ellos a tomar esas clases cuando muchas veces no la necesita y tienen que estudiar muchas otras cosas y no tienen el tiempo de estudiar lenguajes. También hay muchos escuelas secundaria, bueno, muchos universidades tienen requisitos de entrar, de estudiar como dos o tres años de lenguaje en la escuela secundaria. Y por eso, creo que como la mayoría de los estudiantes ya tienen esa experiencia con lenguajes, no necesitan más en la universidad.

Commentary on Sample Response That Earned a Score of 3

This oral response is generally comprehensible but may require the listener's effort to understand the intended meaning because the test taker takes an opposing view against language study: *Creo que no es necesario que todos los estudiantes estadounidenses tienen que estudiar una (un) idioma en la, la universidad.* The test taker then proceeds to say that there are many benefits for the students of a (or "one") language: *como . . . un entendimiento de otra (otro) grupo de gente—todos esos beneficios.* He then goes on to state: *hay unos (unas), ahh, desventajas.* As the test taker continues naming some disadvantages, the listener becomes more aware of the errors in agreement: *Por ejemplo, muchos (muchas) carreras como ingeniería ya tienen muchos cursos, toma mucho tiempo; no la (las) necesita (necesitan) y tienen que estudiar;* and awkward phrasing: *sería muy difícil para ellos a tomar (que ellos tomaran) esas clases.* The vocabulary is adequate and varied, with some idiomatic usage: *tienen que estudiar.* The test taker uses *idioma, lengua,* and *lenguaje* to vary the key word of the response. The concluding sentence strongly conveys his opinion: *creo que como la mayoría de los estudiantes ya tienen esa experiencia con lenguajes, no necesitan más en la universidad.* This is a strong oral response with a natural flow and good pronunciation. The overall sample suggests proficiency and merits a score of 3.

Sample Response 3: Score of 2

Yo creo que todos deben que estudiar un, i, un idioma extranjero. Una razón es que temos, tenemos muchos gente extranjeros aquí que no hablan inglés. Por ejemplo, tengo est, un estudiante en mi clase que no habla inglés bien, y él es en mi clase de español y él tiene problemas con español porque no entiende el inglés. Y con, con gente que puede hablar español, podemos ayudarlo. Dos, la segunda razón. En negocios, es importante que sabemos otros idiomas porque no todos nuestros clientes en el mercado mundial hablan inglés. Si queremos hablar con ellos y comunicar y vender cosas es mejor si podrimos, podríamos hablar su idioma. Ehh, cuando los estudiantes van a otros países, podrían hablar con la gente para, para saber dónde está algunas cosas que quieren ver y, si necesitan algo de emergencia, podrían preguntar por, por ayuda. Para mí, es importante que todos saben más que un, un idiom, idioma, especialmente si es solamente inglés. Necesitan hablar, a lo menos, inglés y español, y para mí, también hablo el idioma de los sordomudos de los Estados Unidos y me gustaría hablar más. Entonces, para mí, sí es importante que todos los estudiantes en la universidad estudian un idioma extranjero.

Commentary on Sample Response That Earned a Score of 2

This speech sample is somewhat comprehensible to a sympathetic listener but may require the listener's effort to understand the intended meaning. The test taker states her opinion: *Yo creo que todos deben que (deben) estudiar un, i, un idioma extranjero.* In stating the reasons for this opinion, the response becomes very repetitive: *Una razón es que temos, tenemos muchos (mucha) gente extranjeros (extranjera) aquí que no hablan inglés. Por ejemplo, tengo est, un estudiante en mi clase que no habla inglés bien, y él es en mi clase de español y él tiene problemas con español porque no entiende el inglés.* The idea is that if people can speak Spanish, they can help native Spanish speakers: *Y con, con gente que puede hablar español, podemos ayudarlo (ayudarla).* The second reason has to do with business, and there the listener becomes aware of the limited control of verbs, especially with the sequence of tenses in complex structures: *En negocios, es importante que sabemos (sepamos) otros idiomas; cuando los estudiantes van (vayan) a otros países, podrían (puedan) hablar con la gente para, para saber dónde está (están) algunas cosas; si necesitan algo de emergencia, podrían (podrán) preguntar por, por (pedir) ayuda.* The lack of correct subjunctive usage continues to be notable: *Para mí, es importante que todos saben (sepan) más que (de) un, un idiom, idioma;* and the conclusion states: *es importante que todos los estudiantes en la universidad estudian (estudien) un idioma extranjero.* The vocabulary is limited, and often repetitive. The test taker has many ideas to express but lacks the control to communicate them correctly. The speech sample starts out poorly but improves toward the end. The limited fluency with satisfactory pronunciation suggests a lack of proficiency and results in a score of 2.

Sample Response 4: Score of 1

Yo creo que es muy importante para estudiantes en la universidads, dades de, ahh, en, la Estados Unidos, amm, estudiar muchas idiomas diferentes de inglés, porque muchas personas en los Estados Unidos son de país diferentes. Ahh, es muy importante para los estudiantes en los Estados Unidos, amm, entienden a otras personas y otras culturas y también cuando estudiantes, amm, limitados a . . . sus educaciones a solamente matemáticas y, umm, otras, uh, sujectos, umm, el personas, los personas no, umm, muy, mmm . . . inteligente. Pero, inteligente no es correcto, pero es importante para los estudiantes, amm, estar más, o, amm, ser más inteligente con otras cosas especialmente como, amm, otras idiomas. Amm, los Estados Unidos es muy popular con otros país para los estudiantes, amm, de otros, amm, países, amm, se, uh, estar en la escuela.

Commentary on Sample Response That Earned a Score of 1

This speech sample is generally incomprehensible even to a sympathetic listener and despite the listener's constant effort to interpret the intended meaning. The test taker is unable to communicate well his reasons for his opinion on the assigned task. After the initial statement of support for the study of foreign languages, there is a breakdown: *Yo creo que es muy importante para (que) (los) estudiantes en la (las) universidads, dades (universidades) de, ahh, en, la (los) Estados Unidos, amm, estudiar (estudien) muchas (muchos) idiomas diferentes de inglés (además del inglés), porque muchas personas en los Estados Unidos son de país (países) diferentes.* There is very little grammatical control and very little vocabulary. The test taker does not have the Spanish language resources to express himself well on the topic. The speech is fragmentary and halting, and there are long pauses. There is virtually no fluency, and pronunciation is only fair. The response clearly demonstrates a lack of proficiency and earns a score of 1.

Constructed-Response Question 5—Sample Responses

We will now look at four scored responses to the fifth constructed-response practice question ("Paraphrase— Legend of the Stars and Moon") and see comments from the scoring leader about why each response received the score it did.

Sample Response 1: Score of 4

Una leyenda hermosa del antiguo México relataba, que hace mucho tiempo, mucho tiempo atrás, había en el cielo y en el firmamento una luna y una serpiente de cristal. Éstas tenían el trabajo de iluminar el mundo. La luna, que era caprichosa, alumbraba cuando quería y si lo hacia, lo hacía muy mal. La serpiente de cristal entonces decidió hacer mejor trabajo. Y corriendo de un lado a otro, alumbraba a todo el mundo. La luna envidiosa, celosa, y caprichosa, al ver que la serpiente de cristal era amada por la gente, le aventó una

> grandísima piedra que la rompió en miles de pedazos. Gracias a esto, el cielo . . .
> es ahora estrellado, y se pueden ver estas hermosos, hermosas estrellas y
> fragmentos de cristal de la serpiente cuando no hay nubes. Son hermosas las
> estrellas.

Commentary on Sample Response That Earned a Score of 4

This oral paraphrase of the Mexican legend is completely and easily comprehensible. The listener rarely needs to make an effort to understand the story line of the legend of the Stars and the Moon: *Una leyenda hermosa del antiguo México relataba, que hace mucho tiempo, mucho tiempo atrás, había en el cielo y en el firmamento una luna y una serpiente de cristal.* The test taker then goes on to describe the Moon and the serpent and the resulting conflict: *La luna, que era caprichosa, alumbraba cuando quería y si lo hacía, lo hacía muy mal. La serpiente de cristal entonces decidió hacer mejor trabajo. Y corriendo de un lado a otro, alumbraba a todo el mundo.* The narrative continues with the description of the jealous Moon throwing a rock to break the crystal serpent into thousands of pieces. The test taker succeeds in completing the narrative by paraphrasing the conclusion: *Gracias a esto, el cielo . . . es ahora estrellado, y se pueden ver estas hermosos, hermosas estrellas y fragmentos de cristal de la serpiente cuando no hay nubes.* The sample has strong grammatical control, with the precise vocabulary of the original version, as well as elaboration. The response shows overall fluency, with a natural rhythm delivered with good pronunciation. The retelling includes almost all of the information, and the content is accurate, which indicates comprehension of oral Spanish. The presentation clearly demonstrates proficiency and merits a score of 4.

Sample Response 2: Score of 3

> Esta leyenda antigua de México se trata . . . de . . . la luna y una serpiente
> preciosa de cristal. Esta leyenda no se sabe de, cuando, cuando pasó
> exactamente en la historia. La luna, lo cual fue muy caprichoza, s . . . brilló a
> veces y el serpiente de cristal siempre . . . quis, quería que hubiera luz. Así es de
> que el serpiente hizo la noche . . . brillar con mucha luz y la luna se, se, no le
> gusto. A la luna no le gustó que siempre había luz y dicidió romper el serpiente
> de cristal en el cielo. Y, la luna arrojó una piedra hacia el serpiente, lo cual no
> pudo escapar . . . o moverse de la pierda y el serpiente se rompió en mil
> pedacitos y los pedacitos son las estrellas.

Commentary on Sample Response That Earned a Score of 3

This oral narrative is generally comprehensible but may occasionally require the listener's effort. The sample includes the basic story without elaboration. The paraphrase is mostly accurate and begins: *Esta leyenda antigua de México se trata . . . de (trata de) . . . la luna y una serpiente preciosa de cristal . . . no se sabe de, cuando, cuando pasó exactamente en la historia.* Then the test taker continues with a sketchy account of the legend, with moderate grammatical control and adequate vocabulary: *La luna, lo (la) cual fue (era) muy caprichoza (caprichosa), s . . . brilló a veces y el (la) serpiente . . . hizo la noche . . . brillar con mucha luz y la luna se, se, no le gusto . . . no le gustó que siempre había luz y dicidió romper el (la) serpiente de cristal en el cielo.* The test taker does not include the information about the Moon being jealous of the serpent's beauty and the affection the people felt for it. The test taker concludes very succinctly: *Y, la luna arrojó una piedra hacia el (la) serpiente, lo cual no pudo escapar . . . o moverse.* There is some difficulty with usage of the preterite and the imperfect and also in agreement: *el (la) serpiente.* Overall, the narrative account is rendered with considerable fluency and good pronunciation and suggests proficiency in completing the task. The response merits a score of 3.

Sample Response 3: Score of 2

> En este pasajé, pasaje hablan de la luna y la serpi, serpiente. La luna y los dos estaban en el cielo pero el serpi, la serpiente estaba muy bellosa y lumbró la noche con su belleza. La luna no lo gustó la serpiente porque estaba muy bonito y tenía la, la, el cariño que los personas . . . le quiso. Porque, por esto, la luna le ventió una pierda a la serpiente y la serpiente quebró en millones y millonas, millones pedazos. Y allí, los pedazos se quedaron en el cielo . . . ¿Por qué, por qué le quebró allí en el cielo? Ese porque tenemos las estrellas y allí los estrellas se quedaron en el cielo para todo los noches que se lumbren mucho . . . y bellosas.

Commentary on Sample Response That Earned a Score of 2

This speech sample of the paraphrase of the legend suggests a lack of proficiency. It is somewhat comprehensible to a sympathetic listener, but errors often interfere with communication. The listener must make an effort to understand the intended meaning: *En este pasajé, pasaje hablan de la luna y la serpi, serpiente.* The test taker does not mention that the passage is about a legend: *La luna y los dos (la luna y la serpiente) estaban en el cielo pero el serpi, la serpiente estaba (era) muy bellosa (bella) y lumbró (alumbró) la noche con su belleza.* It is therefore strange to imagine the Moon together with a serpent who lights up the sky: *(A) la luna no lo (le) gustó la serpiente porque estaba (era) muy bonito (bonita) y tenía la, la, el cariño que los (las) personas . . . le quiso (sentían).* The test taker lacks the grammatical control and the lexical resources to complete the task successfully: *Porque, por esto, la luna le ventió (tiró) una pierda (piedra) a la serpiente y la serpiente (se) quebró en millones y millonas (millones), millones (de) pedazos.* Failure to mention the jealousy of the Moon *(envidiosa)* and the fact that the serpent was *de cristal* lead to difficulty in comprehension. The response indicates limited fluency, with halting speech, and, despite good pronunciation, thus earns a score of 2.

Sample Response 4: Score of 1

> Este historia es eyendo del cómo el cielo fuero formado. Este dices de la historia del sorpiente cristal y como tom, toma, tomó, tomó los piedras del, del mundo, y del, del, umm, del tierre, y se pone in las tierra y se formado de las estrellas. Esa. Es.

Commentary on Sample Response That Earned a Score of 1

This oral presentation is generally incomprehensible even to a sympathetic listener. The speech sample is mostly inaccurate, with very little grammatical control. There are many serious errors in virtually all structures: *Este (esta) historia es eyendo (una leyenda) del (de) cómo el cielo fuero (fue) formado.* The test taker lacks the grammatical and lexical resources to paraphrase the story. It is evident that the level of comprehension is such that the test taker cannot synthesize the information in order to present a cogent retelling of the legend. There is virtually no fluency. The speech is fragmentary and halting, interrupted often by pauses and repetitions: *Este dices (trata) de la historia del (de la) sorpiente (serpiente) (de) cristal y como tom, toma, tomó, tomó los (las) piedras del, del mundo, y del, del, umm, del tierre (tierra), y se pone in (en) las (la) tierra y se formado (forman) de las estrellas.* Despite the listener's constant effort to interpret the intended meaning, the response clearly demonstrates a lack of proficiency. It earns a score of 1.

Constructed-Response Question 6—Sample Responses

We will now look at four scored responses to the sixth constructed-response practice question ("Proposing a Foreign-Student Exchange") and see comments from the scoring leader about why each response received the score it did.

Sample Response 1: Score of 4

> Buenas tardes, distinguidos colegos y colegas de Argentina. Es con un gran placer que les doy la bienvenida a este banquete que hemos preparado aquí, los maestros de "Sherman High School," para Uds. Como maestra secundaria, yo misma . . . es un gran placer para mí tener la oportunidad de hablar con maestros de otros colegios y de otros países. Les propongo que hagamos un entrecambio entre los estudiantes de "Sherman High School" y los estudiantes del "Colegio Sagrado Corazon" en Buenos Aires. He hablado con varios estudiantes aquí en mi "high school" y me han dicho que para ellos sería algo muy emocionante tener estudiantes de Argentina aquí. Para mis estudiantes, yo sé que tener esta oportunidad de hablar cada día con los argentinos, les daría mejor entretenimiento de, o, o, perdón . . . mejor entendimiento de otros países americanos. Mis estudiantes no tienen mucho interés en geografía, pero si tienen amigos que son de otros países, tienen ese interés, y les daría una gran oportunidad.

Commentary on Sample Response That Earned a Score of 4

This oral response demonstrates proficiency. The test taker presents a comprehensible speech to teachers from Argentina, proposing a student-exchange program. This is a complex task that requires a formal register and a special awareness of the audience. The content is accurate and relevant. The speaker begins by addressing the group: *Buenas tardes, distinguidos colegos y colegas de Argentina* and then proceeds to state what a pleasure it is to greet them at the banquet: *Es un gran placer para mí tener la oportunidad de hablar con maestros de otros colegios y de otros países.* Even though these teachers are all from Argentina, the reference is to teachers from "other schools and other countries," which reflects the perspective of the speaker. Grammatical control is evident as the speaker then proposes the exchange: *Les propongo que hagamos un entrecambio (intercambio) entre los estudiantes,* using the indirect command and the subjunctive. The test taker uses a variety of tenses to express his favorable opinion of the program: *He hablado con varios estudiantes aquí en mi "high school" y me han dicho que para ellos sería algo muy emocionante.* The vocabulary is precise and generally idiomatic, though somewhat repetitive: *Para mis estudiantes, yo sé que tener esta oportunidad de hablar cada día con los argentinos, les daría mejor . . . entendimiento de otros países americanos.* The overall fluency and good pronunciation largely determine the score of 4.

Sample Response 2: Score of 3

> Bienvenidos. Los estudiantes . . . pueden beneficiar viviendo con otra familia. Cr, yo creo que es, es necesario . . . para los estudiantes y Uds. son muy importantes porque son maestros. Los estudiantes pueden aprender mucho de Uds. Adema, además, los estudiantes van a vivir exactamente como las familias. Van a comer la misma comida, van a pasar tiempo con la familia, van a viajar con las familias, por las ciudades, y también, van a vivir la vida de . . . las personas en la otra ciudad. Pueden beneficiar todos, los estudiantes y las familias también, porque Uds. pueden aprender de los estudiantes y de su estudiante que va a la otra ciudad, cuando regrese. Yo creo que es una aspecta importante de, de . . . aprender.

Commentary on Sample Response That Earned a Score of 3

This speech sample, though generally comprehensible, occasionally requires the listener's effort to fill in the gaps of what the test taker wants to express. *Bienvenidos* is the simple greeting, and the speaker proceeds to say: *Los estudiantes . . . pueden beneficiar viviendo (beneficiarse por vivir) con otra familia.* The content is mostly accurate and relevant but is presented in simple sentences with repetition: *los estudiantes van a vivir exactamente como las familias. Van a comer la misma comida, van a pasar tiempo con la familia, van a viajar con las familias . . . y tambien, van a vivir la vida de . . . las personas en la otra ciudad.* There is an overall correctness of grammar, but the sample lacks elaboration. The repetition is notable also in its use of the following phrases: *pueden beneficiar viviendo con otra familia; pueden aprender mucho de Uds.; Pueden beneficiar todos; pueden aprender de los estudiantes.* There is also a subjunctive clause: *de su estudiante que va a la otra ciudad, cuando regrese.* The vocabulary is adequate and idiomatic despite the overuse of *ir a* + infinitive and *poder* + infinitive. The oral delivery is sometimes hesitant, but always comprehensible and with good pronunciation. It denotes fluency. The response, because it is mostly accurate and relevant, earns a score of 3.

Sample Response 3: Score of 2

> Buenos días a los estudiantes y visitores de la ciudad de los Estados Nu, Unidos. Los estudiantes de Argentina gustaría nuestra escuela. Los estudiantes de Argentina pueden aprender la cultura, la lengua, y costumbres de los americanos. Entonces, podemos apredien, aprender sus cultura, costumbres, y la lengua. Tendría beneficiar para ambos los paises y los Estados Unidos y Argentino.

Commentary on Sample Response That Earned a Score of 2

This speech sample is somewhat comprehensible to a sympathetic listener but requires the listener's effort to understand the intended meaning. The content is only somewhat accurate in that the greeting—*Buenos días a los estudiantes y visitores (visitantes) de la ciudad (del país) de los Estados Nu, Unidos*—should be directed to the teachers, not to students from the United States. There is limited grammatical control and vocabulary, with unidiomatic word choice: *(A) los estudiantes de la Argentina (les) gustaría nuestra escuela,* which indicates language interference. The test taker does communicate the positive effects of the student exchange: *Los estudiantes de (la) Argentina pueden aprender la cultura, la lengua, y (las) costumbres de los americanos.* He continues with repetition: *podemos apredien, aprender sus (su) cultura, (las) costumbres y la lengua.* In the concluding statement, the listener has to interpret the intended meaning: *Tendría beneficiar para ambos los países y los Estados Unidos y Argentino (Argentina).* The student exchange would benefit both countries—the United States and Argentina. *(El intercambio) tendría beneficios (o habría beneficios) para ambos países, los Estados Unidos y la Argentina.* There is limited fluency, with halting speech and fair pronunciation. The test taker lacks the language resources to communicate the assigned task effectively. This brief sample suggests a lack of proficiency and earns a score of 2.

Sample Response 4: Score of 1

Ben, bienvenidos estudiantes . . . Creo que, que Uds. van a disfrutir nuestra ciudad. Ahhh, hay muchos lugares culturales . . . culturales en esta ciudad y también . . . ahhh, la escuela . . . aquí es muy alta. Es una de las más alta del país.

Commentary on Sample Response That Earned a Score of 1

This speech sample is generally incomprehensible and demonstrates the test taker's lack of ability to fulfill the assigned oral task. The greeting—*Ben, bienvenidos estudiantes*—is directed to the students, not the teachers, and mentions the cultural places in the city: *Creo que . . . van a disfrutir (disfrutar de) nuestra ciudad. Ahhh, hay muchos lugares culturales . . . culturales en esta ciudad.* There is very little vocabulary, and some of that is used inappropriately: *ahhh, la escuela . . . aquí es muy alta. Es una de las más alta del país.* A listener who did not have the test prompt would not really understand what the test taker was talking about. There is virtually no fluency and no elaboration, and the speech is halting, with long pauses. The score for this oral response is 1.

Presentational Writing Section

Constructed-Response Question 7—Sample Responses

We will now look at four scored responses to the seventh constructed-response practice question ("Beach Sequence") and see comments from the scoring leader about why each response received the score it did.

Sample Response 1: Score of 4

La semana pasada hacia un calor horrible. En casa nadie soportaba el calor ni con el aire y los ventiladores auxiliares. Hacia mas calor adentro que afuera. Tomamos la decision de ir con los niños a la playa y aprovechar el sol y la briza del mar. Nos dirigimos en bicicleta y fue un paseo genial. Cuando llegamos a la playa tendimos nuestras toallas y pusimos los parasoles a nuestro alrededor. Nos divertimos muchisimo! Jugamos a la pelota con los niños, nadamos en el mar, tomamos el sol, fue una mañana fenomenal! Ya cuando habia bajado el sol tomamos nuestra merienda encima de una colcha y bajo el parasol. Los emparedados nos supieron a gloria! Ya al anocher nos regresamos a casa en bicicleta. Veniamos contentos de haberla pasado tan bien y satisfechos con la merienda que habiamos comido.

Commentary on Sample Response That Earned a Score of 4

The test taker is asked to tell a story in the past tense according to the scenes shown in six picture frames. This writing sample tells the reader what is going on and, without being able to see the picture sequence, the reader can imagine the situation. The sample is completely comprehensible, with appropriate elaboration. The vocabulary is rich and precise, with the use of idiomatic expressions: *En casa nadie soportaba el calor; Nos dirigimos en bicicleta y fue un paseo genial. (¡)Nos divertimos muchisimo (muchísimo)!* There is grammatical control, with the correct use of the preterite and imperfect verb tenses— despite the troublesome lack of required accents: *hacia (hacía), habia (había), veniamos (veníamos), habiamos (habíamos)*—and also good control of the past perfect, reflexive pronouns, prepositions, and articles. There are some misspellings: *briza (brisa)* and *anocher (anochecer)*. The sample is a coherent, well-organized paragraph that successfully completes the assigned task. There is a flow to the narrative, and the intended meaning is always clear. This sample demonstrates proficiency. It is what the scorers refer to as a "low 4" because, while it is excellent in many ways, it also ignores important conventions of orthography (graphic accents, inverted exclamation marks).

Sample Response 2: Score of 3

La semana pasada había mucho calor y no teníamos el aire acondicionado en nuestra casa, no funciaba. Todos nosotros sudábamos. Decidimos de montar nuestras bicicletas en la playa. Pusimos las toallos en la tierra y una paralluvia (pero parasol) para protegernos del sol. Mi padre y mi hermano jugaron con una pelota de playa, yo nadé en el océano, y mamá leó una novela. Porque teníamos hambre, almorzamos sándwiches y bebimos mucha agua. Alrededor de las cinco de la tarde, regresamos en casa; cada uno puso algo en su bicicleta para ayudar a hacer más fácil el viaje breve. Nos divertíamos este día.

Commentary on Sample Response That Earned a Score of 3

This writing sample is generally comprehensible and only occasionally may require the reader's effort to understand the intended meaning. The sample addresses all of the six pictures in the narrative sequence but without elaboration. The content is relevant, with moderate grammatical control. The verb *había* is used instead of the more idiomatic *hacía mucho calor*. The test taker does use the expression *teníamos hambre* correctly. The vocabulary is adequate but at times awkward. Some errors occasionally interfere with, but do not impede, communication: *funciaba* instead of *funcionaba; leó* should be *leyó; toallos* for *toallas;* the incorrect use of the preposition *en: regresamos en (a) casa;* and the incorrect use of *este* instead of *ese* when referring to the past: *este (ese) día.* There appears to be an attempt at indecisive self-correction, with *pero parasol* for *una paralluvia (un paraguas).* The use of the preterite and imperfect verb tenses is generally correct, with the exception of the fourth picture, where the imperfect could have been used to describe the action as ongoing instead of completed. This writing sample is generally coherent, shows evidence of organization, and suggests proficiency.

Sample Response 3: Score of 2

Fue una dia durante el verano que hacía mucho calor. Habia une familia que estaba sientado en su casa sudiendo porque el aireacondicionado estaba roto. El padre conseguío un idea, para tener toda su familia ir a las playa. La familia estaban de acuerdo y preperó para ir a la playa. La familia montó bicicletas a la playa. La familia traió una para aguas toellas y todo. Los chicos comenzaron a jugar voleybol mientras la hija estuvo nadando. La madre sientó con la paraaguas y leo su libro. Despues de los actividades la familia comió una comida grande y luego regresó a casa. La familia ha cambiado una dia horrible a une dia para recordar.

Commentary on Sample Response That Earned a Score of 2

This sample is somewhat comprehensible to a sympathetic reader, but understanding the intended meaning often requires an effort. The narrative is relevant and addresses all six pictures, but with limited grammatical control. There are error patterns in basic, high-frequency structures, such as agreement between article and noun: *una dia, une dia* should be *un día* (with an accent); *une familia, un idea, los actividades,* and *a las playa* also show incorrect agreement. These error patterns are also evident in the erratic control of verbs: *preperó (preparó), traió (trajo), sientado (sentada), sudiendo (sudando),* as well as the ineffective use of the preterite and imperfect tenses: *estuvo nadando (estaba nadando), leo (leía).* The vocabulary is basic, with a number of misspellings and inconsistencies: *aireacondicionodo (aire acondicionado); una para aguas . . . la paraaguas (un/el paraguas); toellas (toallas); voleybol (voleibol).* There is some idiomatic usage: *hacía mucho calor; estaban de acuerdo,* even though the latter example lacks agreement with the subject, which is a collective noun, *la familia.* There is an inconsistent use of accent marks, with the exception of some regular preterite forms: *montó; comió; regresó.* There is second-language interference, which impedes the flow of the narrative, and the overall lack of control suggests lack of proficiency.

Sample Response 4: Score of 1

La semana pasada, no tuve aire en mi casa. Mis pardes y mi hermana estuvieron muy calor. Entonces, mi papa digo, "Vamos a la playa." Yo tuve mi biceleta, y fui a la playa con mis padres. Mi pa-pa puso una sabaña en la tierra, y mi mamí puso un paraagua en la tierra. Proxmia, yo jugaé con la bola con mi papi. Menitras, mi mama estvo leyendo un libro bajo el paragua, y mi hermana éstvo en el mar. Después de, mi familia tuieron almuzar bajo el paragua. Al fin de día, fuiemos a la casa.

Commentary on Sample Response That Earned a Score of 1

This sample clearly demonstrates a lack of proficiency in writing Spanish. The glaring errors interfere with communication and require the reader's constant effort to interpret the intended meaning. Though the sample attempts to address all of the pictures, the content is often inaccurate, with very little grammatical control. There is an attempt to use the preterite tense, sometimes correctly but awkwardly: *tuve; fui; puso;* but generally incorrectly and where the imperfect should be used: *estuvieron muy calor (tenían mucho calor); yo jugaé (jugaba); mi mama (mamá) estvo leyendo (estaba leyendo); mi hermana éstvo (estaba) en el mar.* The forms *tuieron (tuvieron) and fuiemos (fuimos)* are further evidence of the lack of verb control. There are inconsistencies in spelling: *papa, pa-pa (papá); pardes (padres);* and lack of agreement: *el paragua (el paraguas).* There is an attempt to use connectors, but most are misspelled or incorrect: *proxmia (próxima); menitras (mientras); después de (después); al fin de día (al fin del día).* The second-language interference and many serious errors in virtually all structures indicate that this sample does more than suggest a lack of proficiency. It clearly demonstrates an inability to fulfill the task.

Constructed-Response Question 8—Sample Responses

We will now look at four scored responses to the eighth constructed-response practice question ("Letter—Wooden Plate") and see comments from the scoring leader about why each response received the score it did.

Sample Response 1: Score of 4

Estimados señores,

Les adjunto copia de la nota de compra que realicé en su tienda hace quince días. Como podrán comprobar, la compra fue hecha en su tienda de la calle Mario Molina, en Quito. El objeto que adquirí es un plato de madera labrado a mano. Pagué con mi tarjeta "BISA": les adjunto copia del extracto del banco.

El problema que tengo es el siguiente: el plato ha llegado muy dañado; tiene varios rayones en la parte superior y parte del borde se ha desprendido.

Entiendo que es parte de su responsabilidad el garantizar el envío de los objetos. Por ello les ruego que me envíen otro plato como el que compré. Si no es posible encontrar uno muy semejante—entiendo que al estar hecho a mano puede suceder que no lo hallen—les agradecería que me devolviesen el dinero.

Lamento ocasionarles esta molestia, pero creo que mi petición es comprensible dadas las circunstancias.

Atentamente:

Pablo Ramírez

Commentary on Sample Response That Earned a Score of 4

This sample clearly demonstrates proficiency in the language. It is completely comprehensible. The letter includes most of the assigned tasks, with appropriate elaboration and register. It is accurate and relevant. There is strong grammatical control, with no marked patterns of error. The broad, precise vocabulary is generally idiomatic and varied: *Les adjunto copia de la nota de compra que realicé en su tienda hace quince días . . . El objeto que adquirí es un plato de madera labrado a mano.* The test taker states the problem—*El problema que tengo es el siguiente: el plato ha llegado muy dañado*—and then states what his expectation is to resolve the matter: *les ruego que me envíen otro plato como el que compré.* The sample includes a variety of tenses in the indicative and subjunctive moods: *Como podrán comprobar, la compra fue hecha* (future, then passive voice in preterite) and *les agradecería que me devolviesen el dinero* (conditional and imperfect subjunctive). The letter is completely coherent and well organized, with frequent use of complex sentences. The sample adheres to the appropriate tone and formality of a business letter: *Lamento ocasionarles esta molestia, pero creo que mi petición es comprensible dadas las circunstancias.* Though a more complete heading and date would add to the form of the letter, it is a sophisticated rendering of the task.

Sample Response 2: Score of 3

20 enero, 2001
Artesanías Nacional
1002 Calle Ecuador
Quito, Ecuador 10A14B
Estimados Senores:

Soy Señora Rosa Sanchez. Este verano estuve de vacaciones en Ecuador. Fui a su tienda el veinte de diciembre. Yo compré un plato hermoso de madera. Este plato llegó a mi casa por correo. Pagué por este plato en mi tarjeta de crédito de BISA.

Ahora el plato llegó roto y no sé que hacer. Estoy mandándoles la cuenta de la companía del crédito.

¿Es posible que ustedes puedan mandarme otro plato? ¿Pueden reemplacer el plato?

Muchas gracias por considerar esta sugerencia.
Espero su respuesta,
Señora Sanchez

Commentary on Sample Response That Earned a Score of 3

The sample is generally comprehensible even to a sympathetic reader, although it occasionally requires the reader's effort to understand the intended meaning. While the sample follows the format of a letter, the body is very brief, lacking appropriate elaboration. The test taker includes the assigned tasks, but while the information may be relevant, it is not always accurate: *Este verano estuve de vacaciones en Ecuador. Fui a su tienda el veinte de diciembre.* The reference to summer *(verano)* and the winter date *(el veinte de diciembre)* are valid if one lives in the Southern Hemisphere. Rosa Sanchez states that she is sending the bill from the credit (card) company, but she does not say why: *Estoy mandándoles la cuenta de la companía del (de) crédito.* One infers that it is her proof of purchase and has the pertinent information regarding the transaction. She includes two questions that are redundant: *¿Es posible que ustedes puedan mandarme otro plato?* followed by *¿Pueden reemplacer (reemplazar) el plato?* The sample indicates a moderate control of grammar, with good use of preterite verbs: *estuve; fui; compré; llegó; pagué;* the present progressive: *estoy mandándoles;* and the subjunctive: *que ustedes puedan mandarme.* There are some errors in the use of prepositions: *Pagué por (Pagué); en (con) mi tarjeta; la companía del (de) crédito.* The vocabulary is adequate, with some idiomatic word choice, but occasionally is awkward: *Soy Señora Rosa Sanchez (Soy Rosa Sanchez).* There is evidence of organization but few complex sentences. The sample nevertheless suggests proficiency.

Sample Response 3: Score of 2

> Estimada director de la tienda de cristol,
>
> Me llamo Rosa Sánchez. Fuí en Ecuador para una vacación durante la semana pasada. Yo comprí un plato muy bonito que hizo de manó en su tienda. El trabajador de su tienda en Quito me decía que el plato fue de México y es más antigua. Es un plato café y el cuesto fue $100.00 en la monera americana.
>
> Durante el viaje a los Estados Unidos el plato se rompió. El aeropuerto dijo que fue la falta de la caja que el trabajador de su tienda pusó el plata en. Yo quiero un plato nuevo o el dinero para el plato regresando a mi. Mi direccion es 222 North Beacon Street. Los Angelas, California 90546.
>
> Gracías para su entendamente,
> Rosa Sánchez

Commentary on Sample Response That Earned a Score of 2

This sample is somewhat comprehensible to a sympathetic reader but often requires effort to understand the intended meaning. There is a contradiction in the information given—one sentence states that the plate was handmade in the store: *un plato muy bonito que hizo de manó (fue hecho a mano) en su tienda,* while the following sentence states that the plate was from Mexico and is very old: *el plato fue de México y es más antigua.* There is limited grammatical control, with many errors in basic high-frequency structures. There are errors with verbs: *Fuí (Fui); comprí (compré); decía (dijo); pusó (puso);* and noun errors: *la tienda de cristol (cristal); para una vacación (unas vacaciones); el cuesto (el precio); en la monera (moneda) americana; Mi direccion (dirección); Los Angelas (Los Ángeles); Gracías para (por) su entendamente (entendimiento).* The vocabulary is limited, with word choice that is often unidiomatic and awkward: *El aeropuerto dijo que fue la falta de la caja que el trabajador de su tienda pusó (puso) el plata (plato) en.* There is evidence of second-language interference and the inability to construct complex sentences: *Yo quiero un plato nuevo o el dinero para el plato regresando a mi.* In spite of the errors and English interference, the letter does at least communicate that there is a problem and some expectation of resolution. Overall, however, the sample suggests a lack of proficiency.

Sample Response 4: Score of 1

> Cuando fuí a Ecuador ordene un traste muy bonito. Pide que me lo manden a mi casa. Pero en llegando, la recibe quebrado. Como yo soy uno de sus mejores clientes, quiesera que me manden otro traste con mas cuidado.

Commentary on Sample Response That Earned a Score of 1

This sample clearly demonstrates a lack of proficiency in completing the assigned task. It is not in letter form, with a salutation and closing, and does not include all requested or necessary information—date of purchase, how the transaction was made, the name of the aggrieved party, and where the relacement item is to be sent. There is a marked pattern of lack of control of verbs and accents, which denote the correct tense: *fuí (fui); ordene (ordené); Pide (pedí); recibe (recibí); quiesera (quisiera).* There is an attempt to use the subjunctive, but the verbs should be in the past: *Pide que me lo manden a mi casa (Pedí que me lo mandaran)*. There is awkward vocabulary: *traste* refers to a small glass vase or container, not a plate; and there is also lack of agreement: *la* instead of *lo* in reference to *traste*. The four sentences in Spanish require a sympathetic reader's constant effort to interpret the intended meaning. The combined errors, brevity of the sample, and incompleteness of the task merit a score of 1.

Constructed-Response Question 9—Sample Responses

We will now look at four scored responses to the ninth constructed-response practice question ("Interviewing a Famous Person") and see comments from the scoring leader about why each response received the score it did.

Sample Response 1: Score of 4

First question

> ¿Quién fue la persona que lo motivó para que sobresaliera en esta carrera?

Second question

> ¿Cuáles fueron los obstaculos más difíciles que tuvo que enfrentar?

Third question

> ¿Si usted pudiera cambiar algo en ésta carrera para ser más conocido, que haría?

Fourth question

> ¿Qué mensaje le da a toda esa gente qué quisiera tener su puesto?

Commentary on Sample Response That Earned a Score of 4

This sample demonstrates proficiency in the assigned task of addressing four questions to a dignitary from a Spanish-speaking country. The questions are relevant and indicate strong grammatical control. Question 1 can be answered with a short answer, while questions 2, 3, and 4 may elicit longer answers, such as descriptions, narrations, or opinions. Question 3 could be answered with a short or a long explanation, but the overall complexity of the if-clause structure is taken into account. The initial question mark in question 3 is out of place. It should precede the *que (qué)*. The *¿que (qué) haría?* would most likely elicit an explanation of what one would do in that situation. The use of complex verb structures, especially the imperfect subjunctive, is notable: *para que sobresaliera; Si usted pudiera; qué (que) quisiera*. There is precise, idiomatic vocabulary, with some errors in the use of accents: *obstaculos (obstáculos); ésta (esta) carrera;* and *qué (que) quisiera*. The questions are completely comprehensible, include the appropriate register, *usted*, and thus rate a score of 4.

Sample Response 2: Score of 3

First question

> ¿Por qué decidiste entrar al mundo del espectáculo?

Second question

> ¿Qué a sido algo que crees que te ha fortalezido en tu carrera artística y algo
> que te a costado mucho esfuerzo superar?

Third question

> ¿Qué le dirías a una jóvencita que quiere seguir en los mismos pasos que tú has
> tomado en tu vida? Es decir, que te hubiera gustado que alguien te hubiera
> dicho antes de que tú hubieras entrado a la farandula del Espectáculo?

Fourth question

> ¿Nos podrías comentar sobre lo que estas planeando para el futuro, y si en tus
> planes incluye ayudar a nuestro país a mejorarse educacionalmente,
> economicamente o socialmente?

Commentary on Sample Response That Earned a Score of 3

These four questions are generally comprehensible, though occasionally they may require the reader's effort to understand the intended meaning. The sample includes two questions—1 and 2—that could be answered briefly and two questions—3 and 4—that could elicit longer answers. There is moderate grammatical control, with some irregularities in the verb forms: *a (ha) sido; te ha fortalezido (fortalecido); a (ha) costado;* while *has tomado* is correct. There are a variety of tenses in complex sentences, which, however, are not always correct. Question 3 attempts to clarify the question, but a second convoluted sentence makes it more complicated: *Es decir, que (qué) te hubiera (habría) gustado que alguien te hubiera dicho antes de que tú hubieras entrado . . . ?* There are some errors with accents: *jóvencita (jovencita); estas (estás) planeando;* and errors with the sequence of adverbs: *educacionalmente (educacional); economicamente (económica) o socialmente.* The questions attempt to get some very interesting information, but are worded awkwardly at times. The questions suggest proficiency and merit a score of 3.

Sample Response 3: Score of 2

First Question

> ¿Cuanto tiempo llevas cantando en español?

Second Question

> ¿En tu opinión, cual es la mejor clase de música para bailar?

Third Question

> ¿Qué te gusta mejor, escribir tu música o cantar tu música?

Fourth Question

> ¿Q

Commentary on Sample Response That Earned a Score of 2

This series of questions is comprehensible, but incomplete. It is possible to answer all three questions with short answers, even though questions 2 and 3 are open to elaboration. There is grammatical control but an omission of accents on interrogatives: *cuanto (cuánto)* and *cual (cuál)*. The vocabulary is adequate, with some idiomatic usage: *llevas cantando; qué te gusta?* The use of the informal register, *tú*, is maintained throughout the questions, but the appropriateness of this form is itself open to question. Overall, the sample suggests a lack of proficiency because there are only three questions and each could be answered with a short response. This sample does not successfully fulfill the task and therefore receives a score of 2.

Sample Response 4: Score of 1

First Question

> ¿Que le gusta sobre una estrella?

Second Question

Third Question

Fourth Question

Commentary on Sample Response That Earned a Score of 1

This incomplete sample clearly demonstrates a lack of proficiency. Only one question is presented of the four questions requested concerning the topic. The question is barely comprehensible and its relevance to the task requires a sympathetic reader to interpret the intended meaning. It obviously calls for more inference than one should have to make. The form *le gusta* is correct, with the *le* referring to a formal register, *usted*. Perhaps the use of *ser* would have helped communicate the idea of wanting to know what the famous person likes about being a star. The sample, though incomplete, addresses the topic and is minimally comprehensible. The response barely meets the criteria for a score of 1.

Chapter 11

Are You Ready?—Last-Minute Tips

▶   ▶   ▶   ▶   ▶   ▶   ▶   ▶   ▶   ▶   ▶   ▶

Checklist

Complete this checklist to determine whether you're ready to take the test.

❑ Do you know the testing requirements for your teaching field in the state(s) where you plan to teach?

❑ Have you followed all of the test registration procedures?

❑ Do you know the topics that will be covered in each test you plan to take?

❑ Have you reviewed any textbooks, class notes, and course readings that relate to the topics covered?

❑ Do you know how long the test will take and the number of questions it contains? Have you considered how you will pace your work?

❑ Are you familiar with the test directions and the types of questions for the test?

❑ Are you familiar with the recommended test-taking strategies and tips?

❑ Have you practiced by working through the practice test questions at a pace similar to that of an actual test?

❑ If you are repeating a Praxis Series Assessment, have you analyzed your previous score report to determine areas where additional study and test preparation could be useful?

The day of the test

You should have ended your review a day or two before the actual test date. And many clichés you may have heard about the day of the test are true. You should

- Be well rested

- Take photo identification with you

- Take a supply of well-sharpened #2 pencils (at least three) for the multiple-choice test

- Take blue or black ink pens for the constructed-response test

- Eat before you take the test to keep your energy up

- Be prepared to stand in line to check in or to wait while other test takers are being checked in

You can't control the testing situation, but you can control yourself. Stay calm. The supervisors are well trained and make every effort to provide uniform testing conditions, but don't let it bother you if the test doesn't start exactly on time. You will have the necessary amount of time once it does start.

You can think of preparing for this test as training for an athletic event. Once you've trained, prepared, and rested, give it everything you've got. Good luck.

Appendix A

Study Plan Sheet

▶   ▶   ▶   ▶   ▶   ▶   ▶   ▶   ▶   ▶   ▶   ▶

Study Plan Sheet

See chapter 1 for suggestions about using this Study Plan Sheet.

STUDY PLAN						
Content covered on test	How well do I know the content?	What material do I have for studying this content?	What material do I need for studying this content?	Where could I find the materials I need?	Dates planned for study of content	Dates completed

Appendix B

For More Information

▶ ▶ ▶ ▶ ▶ ▶ ▶ ▶ ▶ ▶ ▶ ▶

Appendix B: For More Information

ETS offers additional information to assist you in preparing for The Praxis Series assessments. *Test at a Glance* materials and the *Registration Bulletin* are both available without charge on our Web site: http://www.ets.org/praxis/index.html.

General Inquiries

Phone: 800-772-9476 or 609-771-7395 (Monday-Friday, 8:00 A.M. to 7:45 P.M., Eastern time)
Fax: 609-771-7906

Extended Time

If you have a learning disability or if English is not your primary language, you can apply to be given more time to take your test. The *Registration Bulletin* tells you how you can qualify for extended time.

Disability Services

Phone: 800-387-8602 or 609-771-7780
Fax: 609-771-7906
TTY (for deaf or hard of hearing callers): 609-771-7714

Mailing Address

ETS—The Praxis Series
P.O. Box 6051
Princeton, NJ 08541-6051

Overnight Delivery Address

ETS—The Praxis Series
Distribution Center
225 Phillips Blvd.
Ewing, NJ 08628